# Dead FEMINISTS

## historic HEROINES

IN Living color

## Chandler O'LEARY & Jessica SPRING

With→ FOREWORD BY JILL LEPORE

SASQUATCH
SEATTLE

Printed in China

Published by Sasquatch Books
20 19 18 17 16          9 8 7 6 5 4 3 2 1

Editor: Hannah Elnan
Production editor: Em Gale
Design: Anna Goldstein
Illustration and lettering: Chandler O'Leary
Endsheets: Jessica Spring
Copyeditor: Jessyca Murphy

Library of Congress Cataloging-in-Publication Data is available.

ISBN: 978-1-63217-057-6

Sasquatch Books
1904 Third Avenue, Suite 710
Seattle, WA 98101
(206) 467-4300
www.sasquatchbooks.com
custserv@sasquatchbooks.com

**For my sisters**

—Jessica Spring

**For aimée M-A**

—Chandler O'Leary

*What's an angel?*
*I'd rather be a woman.*

—WONDER WOMAN

# Contents

❖ ❖ ❖

# Foreword

❖ ❖ ❖

In 1853 Sarah Josepha Hale, the editor of *Godey's Lady's Book*, published an enormous nine hundred–page compilation of biographies and portraits of famous women. She called it *Woman's Record: Or, Sketches of all Distinguished Women, from "the Beginning" till A.D. 1850. Arranged in Four Eras. With Selections from Female Writers of Every Age*. It had taken her three years to write it. She dedicated it to "The Men of America," that they might learn something by it, about what a woman can do:

> To show what she has done, I have gathered from the records of the world the names and histories of all distinguished women, so that an exact estimate of the capabilities of the sex might be formed by noting what individuals have accomplished through obstacles and discouragements of every kind.

The engravings, by the New York firm of Lossing and Barritt, were cut into wood and printed in black and white (the firm's name hides a female engraver: John Lossing's daughter Helen worked in the shop). Hale explained that the Lossing and Barritt portraits, "besides their usefulness in stamping on the mind of the reader a more permanent impression of each individual character thus illustrated, furnish an interesting study to the curious in costume and the adept in taste."

Portrait galleries of famous women have appeared, regularly, ever since. One of my favorites is "The Wonder Women of History," a four-page centerfold that appeared in every issue of Wonder Woman comics, from 1942 to 1947. Chandler O'Leary and Jessica Spring's wonderful collection, Dead Feminists, is in this same tradition. So far as I can tell, Sappho is about the only woman who appears in both *Dead Feminists* and *Woman's Record*; Dolley Madison is one of the few women who appeared in Hale's collection and became a Wonder Woman of History too. Every age names its own greats.

Sarah Josepha Hale wasn't shy about the importance of compiling collections of biographies and portraits of women. "No work extant is similar to mine," she told readers of her book, "for this reason, I am sure it will be welcomed. The world wants it."

A very warm welcome, too, to *Dead Feminists*. The world wants it.

**—JILL LEPORE**

Cambridge, Massachusetts
November 2015

Introduction

Collaborate

# WOMEN WE CAN BELIEVE IN

It was 2008. The presidential election was on the horizon, and whatever the outcome, we knew the election was going to make history. After the primaries, it was clear that the winning team would have one member who was not a white man, for the first time ever. The election commentary was brutal, often focusing on the women candidates and how they looked—and for one candidate, undue attention was given to her eyeglasses, even from liberal media. Jessica Spring, a letterpress artist in Tacoma, Washington, spent many days in her print shop during the election season listening to the gory details dissected on liberal public radio, and poured her frustration into her work. She dug up a quote by suffragist Elizabeth Cady Stanton that—despite being written before the turn of the last century—summed it all up: "Come, come my conservative friend, wipe the dew off your spectacles and see the world is moving."

Chandler O'Leary, an illustrator and letterer, had just moved to town, ready to take the leap to full-time self-employment. Serendipitously she discovered that fellow type aficionado Jessica lived right up the street. Both transplants with experience in the Midwest graphic design and letterpress worlds, we bonded over shared frustration with the election and appreciation for the printed word. Jessica painstakingly hand-sets vintage metal and wood type to create artwork that combines text and image. Chandler uses drawing as a tool to create original type and give words a unique voice. We both spend a fair amount of time writing, including original text in our work and penning articles and blog posts. We discovered that we both have a background in graphic design and printmaking—and that we share a common love for the art of the broadside.

Jessica asked Chandler to provide an illustration for the Elizabeth Cady Stanton print that would reference Sarah Palin's infamous eyewear and give us both a way to throw our support behind Barack Obama. In no time at all, Chandler had sketched the glasses . . . and a lot more. Every word of Stanton's quote was hand-drawn letter by letter, surrounded by detailed borders, curlicues, and even the suffragist's portrait. Having no idea how people might respond to the print, we agreed on a small but meaningful edition of

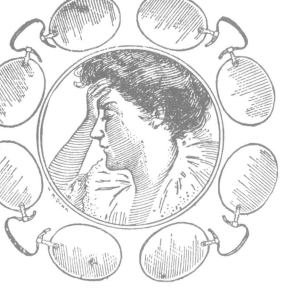

forty-four copies, in honor of the next (forty-fourth) president. We capped off the piece with a colophon, a short passage of text including biographical details for Stanton and production notes about the artwork. While printing we made a quick decision to make a two-color design, cutting up the printing plate on the fly, and delighting in the end result. The finished product was a combination of careful design and improvisation by the seat of our pants—and somehow it worked. The response to the print, especially from women, was overwhelmingly positive, and Obama's victory was made even sweeter by our participation, however indirect. That feeling of "printer's high" inspired us to keep working together and create another broadside in the same format, including another quote by a woman to support a cause we believed in. We had no idea at the time that we were launching a series, but the way we shared ideas, tasks, and expertise turned into a collaboration that would continue for many years.

## BROADS AND BROADSIDES

Throughout history artists have acted as a sort of mirror for society, responding to and reflecting upon the cultures in which they live and work. This can take a wide variety of forms, from deliberately political pieces to scenes of everyday life, and everything in between. Artists are people with beliefs and biases like anybody else—we just happen to have the tools and the desire to set down our thoughts with pen or brush. In our separate work we are artists who make images and who have strong opinions that can play a part in the art we make. It wasn't until we came together as a team, though, that we channeled our beliefs into something greater.

Broadsides, or broadsheets, can be called the great-grandmothers of the modern poster. A large sheet of paper typically printed on one side only, the broadside was used to promote political causes, spreading the word on the street. Common between the sixteenth and nineteenth centuries in the Western world, broadsides could be simple advertisements, news proclamations, or a format for printing ballads. Early printers and writers at that time took advantage of this to disseminate information quickly to as many people as possible. The democratization of printing hundreds of years ago led to inexpensive books being produced, which in turn brought literacy to a greater percentage of the population. Today the media of mass communication has moved on, but the broadside is still a format employed by printers—it's evolved into an art form that still uses text as its main conceptual and design tool.

In creating artwork together, we wanted to hearken back to the original purpose of the broadside: this idea of posters as rabble-rousers. Putting our broadsides online has mirrored the original democratization of early printing. We're still creating a physical object, but by posting bills online (instead of on a tree or in the town square) and through people sharing our work on platforms like social media, we're spreading the word in a way that parallels what those early printers were doing. One notable difference today is gender: when broadsides were

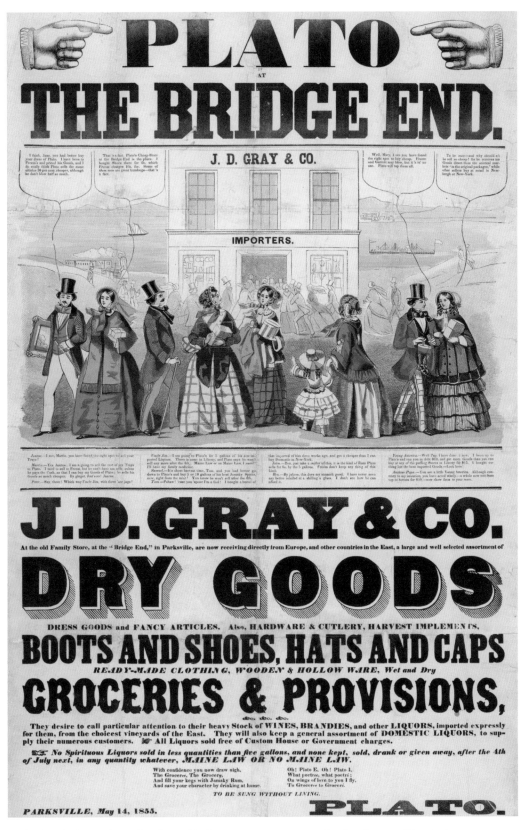

▲ The broadside was the earliest form of both mass communication and political protest. Historical figures used them to spread the word about their causes, and bring about sweeping social change.

first popularized, it was men who manned the presses. Now we're seeing a major cultural shift: women are dominating the ranks of printers today. As artists and entrepreneurs we are part of a community of women that is both supportive and staggering in size. And in the grand tradition of those early firebrands, we've left a trail of broadsides in our wake, forging our path with the printed word.

## A WOMAN IS THE TICKET

An essential part of our collaboration has been negotiating details of what our series would be, the rules of engagement that guide our decisions. The most obvious requirement was to choose a woman to quote as the jumping-off point for the piece, and a deceased one at that. While there are many women in history whom we admire, often they don't have a quote that works for a broadside because of length, antiquated language, or the simple fact that their words weren't recorded. There are lots of voluble politicians and writers with plenty of words on record, but we also value the search for those women who didn't have a platform for their voices. Representing a broad variety of women has been our ongoing goal: highlighting different races and cultures as well as periods in history, hopefully all tied to contemporary concerns. This has been a big challenge for us—as white women attempting to portray difference, without the benefit of being "real" historians or academics. Finally, we actively avoid quotes that denigrate men or even compare women to men, in an attempt to move beyond "we can do anything men can do!"—while also avoiding the use of *man* or *men* as a stand-in for all of humanity.

Another important aspect of the project has been by virtue of its name. Jessica came up with the nickname "Dead Feminists," which we used casually to refer to our project, but it took serious persuasion from Chandler to make it official. While it started slightly tongue-in-cheek—especially as many of the women we've profiled have themselves denied being feminists—we wanted to own the word *feminist*. By using it openly we want the term to stand for women who are independent, who speak out in defense of whatever they believe, and who live a life of purpose (and if their cause aligns with our progressive social and political values, it's a bonus, but not a necessity). We embrace a literally broad definition of *feminism*, but an active version where we can move beyond "women are awesome!" to a greater focus on equal rights and opportunities, everywhere, for everyone. After all the world is full of inspirational pieces quoting Dead White Men, but our foremothers didn't garner nearly the same attention as our forefathers.

# N W P C   A WOMAN IS THE TICKET

*Bella Abzug*

◄ A campaign pennant featuring the slogan of the National Women's Political Caucus, signed by Congresswoman Bella Abzug (D-NY).

Coming out publicly as feminists has been cathartic for us as well. While printing might now be female dominated, the related fields of typography and graphic design are still predominately male. That often leaves us in the position of having to explain ourselves, rather than simply letting our work speak for itself. Any artist faces a constant challenge to take a spark of an idea, a creative moment, and then gather the skills and determination to make that idea emerge into something tangible. As women artists, we often fight the additional battle to be taken seriously, responding to unsubtle remarks about our "hobbies," and being consistently questioned about the worth of our work, particularly in a world that sees more value in more handsomely remunerated male-dominated professions. Having the words of our foremothers to look back upon reminds us that we're not the first to fight this fight—nor will we be the last.

▲ Taking the phrase *Girl Power* literally.

# GETTING OUR HANDS DIRTY

Our collaboration has always been fairly fluid, with both of us involved in some degree with every aspect of the process. We have an ongoing list of women we'd like to feature or quotes that inspire us, waiting for the right social cause to champion. Jessica typically researches the women we profile, gathering enough information for the colophon, with additional details to expand upon on the blog. Chandler is the illustrator, combining biographical details with cues from each woman's era for inspiration. The first step involves creating a very rough pencil sketch with enough detail to discern a concept or open up discussion: from "you should add a giant octopus" to other seemingly crazy ideas that somehow make their way into the drawing. Chandler's final illustration usually has some fairly refined ideas of color and color layering, but those can change when Jessica actually mixes the ink, based on nebulous suggestions like a tasty persimmon. We work especially closely at this point because, despite the best-laid plans, everything can change as ink hits paper and colors react to one another. It's also the time when something imagined, or even roughly viewed via a computer screen, can become a whole other thing with the alchemy of printing. Once we've agreed on how everything looks, Jessica prints the edition. Chandler launches the new work via social media and blog posts, giving readers more insight into the women

▼ The photos below detail our process, step by step. Each of our broadsides begins with Chandler's hand-lettered drawings, which we then convert into photopolymer plates for printing. Each color on the finished broadside is hand-mixed and requires a separate printing plate.

▼ Jessica prints each broadside by hand on an antique Vandercook proofing press. She prints each color pass separately, carefully aligning each plate with the one previous. The broadside pictured below is made up of four layers of ink, precisely registered to comprise the full-color illustration.

and issues we profile. As artists who usually work alone, it has been really fun and rewarding to combine our skills in a way that allows our two halves to make a much better whole.

Our method in creating the Dead Feminists series is a mix of traditional and contemporary letterpress processes. Historical broadsides were printed with metal and wood type composed to create a form for printing (as Jessica does with her other projects). Our series is completely hand-drawn using original illustrations and typography, which reference historical examples from the time period in which each feminist lived. Chandler designs the layout in pencil, and then redraws it in black ink, separating the colors by hand. Then we scan the final version into a digital file to create photopolymer plates, easily placed on a base to create a raised surface from which Jessica can print. Every color in the print is represented by a different plate and pass through the press which must be carefully registered or lined up. When plates are overlapped, the two colors combine to create another color. Each design has a minimum of two colors, some with as many as five. We're constantly pushing the envelope with tight registration, detail work, large floods (covering the whole sheet with ink) and some experimentation (as explained in more detail in the captions that accompany the reproductions throughout this book).

## THE COLLABORATION GROWS

Over the course of our collaboration we have chosen quotes that illuminate the social issues that affect women. We've been able to share the success of the project in small ways from the beginning by contributing prints and postcards to support fundraisers from school auctions to arts organizations. Over the years we have

| Sappho born | | Jane Mecom born | | Harriet Tubman born | | Lili'uokalani born | |
|---|---|---|---|---|---|---|---|
| 630 to 612 BCE | circa 800 | 1712 | 1815 | 1822 | 1836 | 1838 | 1848 |
| | Fatima al-Fihri born | | Elizabeth Cady Stanton born | | Battle of the Alamo | | Emma Smith DeVoe born |

| Virginia Woolf born | | Eleanor Roosevelt born | | Rachel Carson born | | Babe Zaharias born | |
|---|---|---|---|---|---|---|---|
| 1882 | 1883 | 1884 | 1885 | 1907 | 1910 | 1911 | 1917 |
| | Imogen Cunningham born | | Alice Paul born | | Elizabeth Zimmermann born | | Gwendolyn Brooks born |

also spoken about our series around the United States, highlighting printing as a particularly important form of "women's work." In 2010, after researching a new broadside at our state library in the midst of massive funding cuts, we committed to donating a portion of funds from the sale of each broadside from that point on, supporting nonprofits that had aligning values. In most cases we are able to find organizations that work on a very small scale within their communities, where our small donation would be meaningful. While it may not be much, if we all lift a little, the burden is eased.

When the opportunity arose to write this book, we were inspired to collaborate on a larger scale both with our publisher and a local community foundation. With their help we've seeded a foundation, watered with proceeds from the sale of each book, and fertilized with contributions from friends who have supported us throughout the project. The Dead Feminists Fund will support small grassroots nonprofits that align with our mission of empowering women and girls to become a force for good in their own communities. A portion of future broadside and book sales will continue to support the fund, along with contributions from donors.

We hope you'll join our collaboration, continuing the work done by all these inspiring women. In the words of Eleanor Roosevelt, "It is better to light a candle than curse the darkness."

| | Thea Foss born | | Adina De Zavala born | | Dr. Cora Smith Eaton born<br>Marie Curie born | | Sarojini Naidu born | |
|---|---|---|---|---|---|---|---|---|
| 1857 | 1860 | 1861 | 1863 | 1867 | 1869 | 1879 | 1881 |
| | May Arkwright Hutton born<br>Annie Oakley born | | Emancipation Proclamation<br>issued by President Lincoln | | Emma Goldman born | | Bernice Sapp born |

| 19th Amendment ratified and<br>American women gain the vote | | Shirley Chisholm born | | Sadako Sasaski born | | National Organization for<br>Women (NOW) is founded | |
|---|---|---|---|---|---|---|---|
| 1920 | 1923 | 1924 | 1929 | 1943 | 1964 | 1966 | 2015 |
| | Alice Paul writes the original<br>Equal Rights Amendment | | Rywka Lipszyc born | | Civil Rights Act is enacted<br>into law | | US Supreme Court upholds<br>same-sex marriage nationwide |

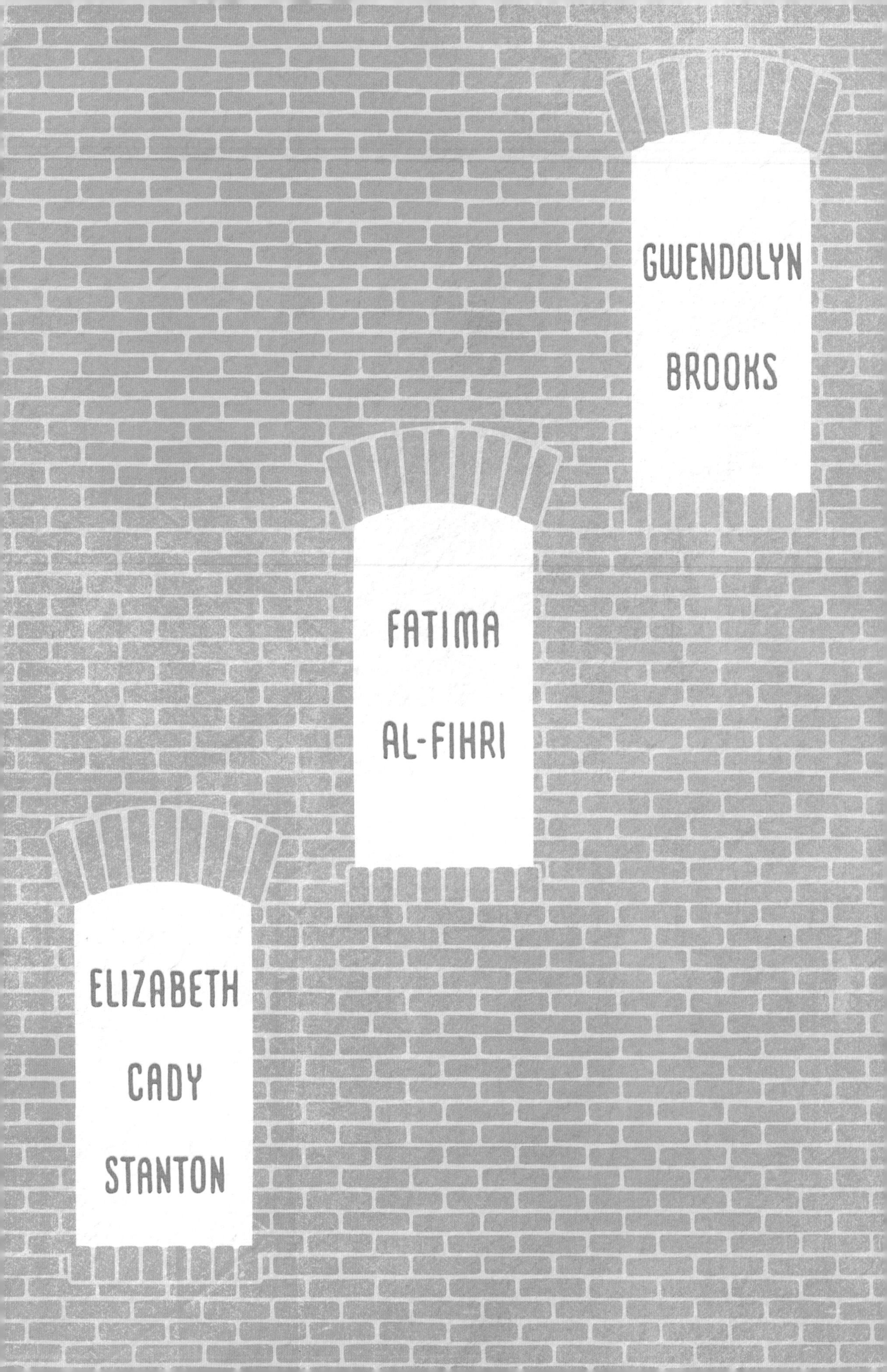

GWENDOLYN

BROOKS

FATIMA

AL-FIHRI

ELIZABETH

CADY

STANTON

*Chapter 1*

# BUILD

With a profound respect for education and the opportunities it provides, these women all spent their lives building their communities. One woman constructed a movement, one raised a place of worship, and another used words to build character.

# ELIZABETH CADY STANTON

Born Elizabeth Cady on November 12, 1815, in Johnstown, New York ✦ Her most often delivered speech, "Our Girls," encouraged young women to get an education ✦ Married Henry Stanton with a ceremony that omitted "obey," followed by a honeymoon at the World Anti-Slavery Convention ✦ Helped organize the first-ever women's rights convention in Seneca Falls, New York ✦ President of the National Woman Suffrage Association for twenty years ✦ Died in New York in 1902, eighteen years before women achieved suffrage

While some women take a lifetime to recognize their path in life, Elizabeth Cady Stanton had the motivation to build a movement at a very young age. She was eleven years old, one of five girls in the family, when her only brother died. Her father's response as he comforted young Stanton: "Oh, my daughter, I wish you were a boy!" Determined to prove she was every bit "as good as a boy," she studied Greek, Latin, and higher mathematics—subjects normally reserved for men. Barred from Union College, she attended Troy Female Seminary instead, excelling in speech and debate. These skills were critical in writing the Declaration of Sentiments, modeled on the Declaration of Independence and signed by attendees at the 1848 women's rights convention at Seneca Falls.

Stanton built awareness with her readers and audiences, highlighting not just women's inability to vote, but also their subservient role in society. Following the Seneca Falls Convention, Stanton hit the lecture circuit eight months of each year from 1848 to 1860. Unlike the audiences at suffrage conventions, these were regular small-town folks, and Stanton's approach was apolitical, carefully weaving motherly advice and entertaining personal stories about her own children. She would question standards of beauty and fashion that demanded women endanger their health with corsets, hoops, and high heels that limited their mobility and opportunities. Lectures would conclude with a vision of what the world *could* be for girls: "The coming girl is . . . to hold an equal place with her brother in the world of work, in the colleges, in the state, the church, and the home." In many ways Stanton's message was far more revolutionary than the call for suffrage, confronting firmly held customs and traditions.

Much of Stanton's suffrage work was done in partnership with Susan B. Anthony, who was more well-known but benefited from Stanton's mastery as a speechwriter. Together they published *The Revolution*, a weekly newspaper and the official voice of the National Woman Suffrage Association. Unlike mainstream publications, they covered topics of interest to women including sex education, domestic violence, divorce, reproductive rights, unionization, and discrimination against female workers.

Though she spent her life on gaining suffrage for women, Stanton died without ever casting a ballot. Today she is remembered not just for her efforts on behalf of suffrage, but as one of the primary architects of the women's rights movement.

▲ Stanton's partnership with Anthony lasted fifty years. Stanton once wrote to her friend: "No power in heaven, hell or earth can separate us, for our hearts are eternally wedded together."

▶ Suffrage was not the only cause Stanton championed. She also helped pass the Women's Property Bill, one of many state laws enacted to grant married women the right to own property.

**S**tanton is honored today in the pantheon of suffragists, so it's easy to forget how controversial she was in her day. Her unorthodox views on religion, birth control, and women's employment were years ahead of her time—and unpopular even with her fellow activists. One major rift she caused was with the abolitionist movement. Stanton, an ardent abolitionist herself, campaigned for simultaneous, universal suffrage for both women and freed Blacks. However, her views and occasional use of racist rhetoric brought her to loggerheads with her former ally Frederick Douglass, who viewed women's rights as a distraction from the more urgent issue of suffrage for Black men. Douglass's cause found resolution first with the passage of the Fifteenth Amendment in 1870; it took another fifty years for women of any race to achieve parity at the ballot.

The controversies stirred up by Stanton echo modern politics and the persistent belief that only one cause or human right can be fought for at a time. Intersectional feminism may not have had a name in Stanton's era, but the issues it encompasses are now coming to the fore of modern politics. Today's voters still hear the refrains *America isn't ready for a woman president* or *equal pay is impossible in this economy* or *same-sex marriage is not a civil right*. This is why we chose Stanton for our very first broadside. Of course it made sense to feature a suffragist in a piece initially timed with the 2008 presidential election—but more than that, Stanton taught us that a woman's right to vote is more important than ever these days, in a world where some women still don't have that right or that right is abridged. As long as marginalized groups and inequality remain in our society, it is vital that *every* cause and community is built with a foundation of empowered and enfranchised voters.

*Puck*

**AN ANTI-SUFFRAGE VIEWPOINT**

DRAWN BY W. E. HILL

GAYLORD (*in cafe dansant*): There's my wife! And I'll bet she's looking for me!
FAIR COMPANION: Oh, dear! Why can't some people understand that woman's place is in the home?

▲ While anti-suffrage campaigns targeted women in the late nineteenth and early twentieth centuries, today's voter ID laws disenfranchise many elderly, poor, minority, immigrant, and disabled voters.

▲ Foundational garments were also the target of Stanton's speeches, as she questioned their ill effects on women's health

➤ It took nearly a century to achieve women's suffrage in the United States—yet in the 2008 presidential election, only around 65 percent of women voters cast a ballot.

▲ The list of Stanton's friends and colleagues reads like a "Who's Who" of early American feminism. Among her collaborators were Lucretia Mott, Lucy Stone, and Sojourner Truth.

◄ In 1895 Stanton published *The Woman's Bible*, calling into question the role of religion in oppressing women: "I know no other books that so fully teach the subjection and degradation of woman."

*1* Broadside design and lettering are informed by the era in which our feminists lived. Here we took inspiration from Victorian ephemera.

*2* Originally designed as a one-color broadside, we changed ink colors on the fly, cutting up the plate to create a two-color print.

*3* A portrait of each feminist is included on her broadside. Stanton's likeness is done in the style of vintage circus posters.

*4* Buried in the illustration is a nod to the infamous spectacles that started it all for us.

*5* The manicule, also called the index or fist, is used to highlight or direct the flow of text.

*6* *Come, Come* is a vintage play on the modern political poster—our way of throwing our proverbial hat into the ring.

## "Come, come my conservative friend, wipe the dew off your spectacles and see the world is moving."

### COME, COME

*No. 1 in the series*

**YEAR CREATED:** *2008*

**ISSUE:** *In recognition of the right—and responsibility—to vote*

**EDITION:** *Forty-four prints; the election of the forty-fourth president of the United States*

**DONATION:** *No donations made this early in the series*

COME, COME MY CONSERVATIVE friend WIPE THE DEW OFF YOUR SPECTACLES AND SEE THE WORLD IS ALL MOVING.

~ELIZABETH CADY STANTON~

Elizabeth Cady Stanton (1815—1902) spent her life in pursuit of women's rights. She wrote many speeches delivered by Susan B. Anthony, who said Stanton "forged the thunderbolts" that she delivered as they worked together for women's suffrage. Stanton raised seven children and organized the first women's rights convention in Seneca Falls, NY in 1848 but died without ever casting her vote before the 19th Amendment passed in 1920.

Illustrated by Chandler O'Leary and printed by Jessica Spring in recognition of a woman's right and responsibility to vote. 44 copies were printed by hand at Springtide Press in Tacoma before the election of 2008.

CHANDLER OLEARY                    31/44

# FATIMA AL-FIHRI

Born circa 800 in Kairouan, Tunisia ✦ Named for one of the four Women of First Rank in Islam, the Prophet's fourth daughter ✦ Her family migrated to Morocco during the reign of King Idris II, who was known as a champion of education ✦ Founded University of al-Qarawiyyin, while her sister founded al-Andalus mosque nearby ✦ Died circa 880; remembered as a symbol of generosity and faith

Fatima al-Fihri* lived so long ago—in a time and place where women's biographies were not recorded—that we know very little about her life. Her place in history has become the stuff of legend rather than verifiable fact. Yet al-Fihri left behind an enormous legacy—one that was so real and generous as to ensure she will never be forgotten.

Al-Fihri and her sister Miriam grew up in the city of Fez. Now nicknamed the "Athens of Africa," Fez has been the cultural and spiritual hub of the region for centuries (as well as Morocco's political capital until 1925). King Idris II, a former child prodigy and a highly educated ruler, united the city under Islamic culture, establishing a stable monarchy and flourishing commercial capital. As a well-educated woman herself, al-Fihri felt strong ties to her community and wished to enhance its intellectual significance.

After the death of her father, al-Fihri vowed to spend her entire inheritance on building a mosque—which, as the cornerstone of the community, was both a place of worship and a center of learning. In 859 she founded al-Qarawiyyin, which operated in a way similar to a modern university. Al-Qarawiyyin offered courses in grammar, rhetoric, logic, medicine, mathematics, astronomy, chemistry, history, geography, and music—creating well-rounded scholars and attracting brilliant minds from around the world. Notably, women were not allowed to attend. One of the largest mosques in Africa and an educational center of the Islamic world, al-Qarawiyyin is considered the oldest university still in operation. Though the details of her life have been forgotten, al-Fihri's gifts have created a ripple effect that can be felt today, centuries later.

---

* No surviving portraits of al-Fihri exist to our knowledge. This is an historical photo of a North African Muslim woman.

▲ Non-Muslim scholars studied at al-Qarawiyyin, including Gerbert of Auvergne, credited with introducing the concept of zero to Europe. Artist Suzanne Moore explored zeros at Springtide Press.

◄ Al-Qarawiyyin is not just the oldest university, it was also the world's first degree-granting educational institution. Courses from mathematics to medicine are still taught as they were when it began.

▲ Since al-Qarawiyyin is the only physical evidence of her life, it is the focal point of our broadside.

Our path to discovering al-Fihri began in April 2014, when more than two hundred girls were kidnapped from their school in Chibok, Nigeria. In the aftermath the media was filled with accusations leveled at Islam—a culture that actually has a long history of valuing education and knowledge. We also know that the danger of extremism knows no cultural boundary—and that it would benefit us all to build a world where every girl has the opportunity and security to obtain an education.

We took great care with our research for this piece—after all, we were attempting to portray with sensitivity a culture very different from our own. Yet still we had many questions and doubts. After all we had to go back twelve hundred years to find a woman like al-Fihri, who was remembered for her deeds. Despite our best attempts, we could not find a direct quote by any historical Muslim woman that was relevant to education. Most difficult of all for us is the fact that al-Fihri herself could never have attended the university she founded—only just recently has admission opened to women. So creating this piece—painstakingly drawing and printing it by hand—became a meditative exercise in trying to understand.

While one broadside—or this book—won't completely answer the complex questions unraveling in the Middle East, we do know we have to keep asking and continue learning. What we do know is this: *every* human life has worth. The best chance anyone can have to build a good life is to obtain an education. Knowledge is the best defense we know against extremism, poverty, and violence. So this is where we begin—where we should *always* begin.

▲ To help ensure the safety and quality of girls' education worldwide, we donated a portion of our proceeds to Girl Up, a nonprofit campaign of the United Nations Foundation that assists some of the world's hardest-to-reach adolescent girls.

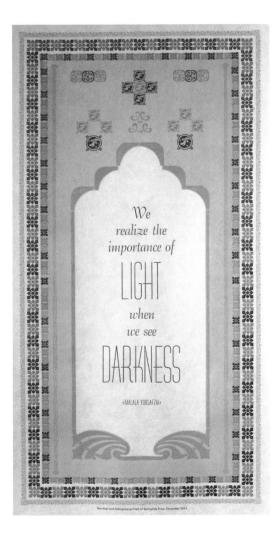

We
realize the
importance of
LIGHT
when
we see
DARKNESS

+MALALA YOUSAFZAI+

Handset and letterpress printed at Springtide Press. November 2013

◄ Al-Fihri's legacy of honoring education continues through modern Muslim women like Malala Yousafzai, who is quoted here on a hand-set broadside Jessica printed.

▲ As the world's first true melting-pot culture, the Islamic world has a long history of innovation, education, and the spreading of ideas that made their way to medieval Europe.

▼ From art and architecture to medicine and science, many of the concepts we take for granted—such as algebra, chemical processes, and the practice of psychiatry—were brought to Europe by Muslim scholars.

*1* Arabesques are a fundamental element of Islamic art, used extensively to inspire typographic ornamentation.

*2* Our print is dominated by an Islamic tile design, based on a geometric pattern of five- and ten-point stars.

*3* The color scheme is related to that of the real structures of al-Qarawiyyin, especially the famous green roof tiles.

*4* We also included *Kufic* script (a style of Arabic calligraphy), which decorates the mosque al-Fihri founded.

*5* The *Basmala* is a common calligraphic motif in Islam, which translates to "In the name of Allah, Most Gracious, Most Compassionate."

*6* Because it is forbidden to create images of Allah or the Prophet in Islam, pictorial calligraphy is often used instead.

## Oum al Banine
## (Mother of the Children)

## THE VEIL OF KNOWLEDGE

*No. 20 in the series*

**YEAR CREATED:** *2014*

**ISSUE:** *The right and necessity for every girl and woman to receive an education*

**EDITION:** *125.4 prints; this number is the solution to an equation we devised out of numbers that are highly symbolic in Islam*

**DONATION:** *Girl Up*

MOTHER of the Children · Oum al Banine · Oum al Banine · MOTHER of the Children

Oum al Banine · Oum al Banine

Mother of the Children · Oum al Banine · Mother of the Children

Fatima al-Fihri

Mother of the Children · Mother of the Children

Mother of the Children · Oum al Banine

Oum al Banine · Oum al Banine

Mother of the Children

Oum al Banine · Oum al

Mother of the Children

Oum al Banine · Oum

Fatima Al-Fihri (c. 800 – 880)
grew up in Fez, Morocco with her sister
Miriam, daughters of a wealthy Tunisian
merchant. The daughters were well-educated and devoted
to their community. After the death of their father, Fatima
vowed to spend all her inheritance in building a mosque,
both a place for worship and a center of learning. In
859, she founded Al-Qarawiyyin which offered courses
in grammar, rhetoric, logic, medicine, mathematics, astronomy, chemistry, history, geography and music – drawing
scholars and students from all over the world. (Gerbert
of Auvergne – later Pope Sylvester II – studied there, and
was credited with the introduction of Arabic numbers
and the concept of zero to Europe.) This important
spiritual and educational center of the Islamic world,
one of the largest mosques in Africa, is considered the
oldest university still in operation. As a woman with
such generosity and vision, Fatima is remembered and
honored as Oum al Banine, "the mother of the children."

Illustrated by Chandler O'Leary and printed by
Jessica Spring, with the knowledge that all women must
have the right to an education. 125.4 copies were
printed by hand at Springtide Press in Tacoma.

July 2014

CHANDLER O'LEARY          8/125.4

# GWENDOLYN BROOKS

Born Gwendolyn Elizabeth Brooks on June 7, 1917, in Topeka, Kansas ✦
Her poetry appeared in *American Childhood* when she was just thirteen; by
age seventeen, was published regularly in the *Chicago Defender* ✦ Awarded the
Pulitzer Prize for Poetry in 1950 for her book *Annie Allen*, the first Black*
person so honored ✦ Awarded more than eighty honorary degrees ✦
Illinois poet laureate for thirty-two years, until her death in 2000

As one of our most beloved and notable American poets, Gwendolyn Brooks spent her life building a legacy of poetry that fearlessly tackles issues of race, gender, and class. Gwendolyn grew up in Chicago; her father was a janitor and her mother a teacher. Brooks started writing poetry early and was encouraged by poet Langston Hughes both to study modern poetry and write as much as possible. She followed his advice by garnering a weekly column in a Chicago newspaper by 1934. Her first book of poetry, *A Street in Bronzeville*, was published by Harper & Row in 1945 and brought acclaim that included her first Guggenheim Fellowship.

While raising two children, Brooks continued to write poetry in both traditional and experimental forms, creating memorable characters leading ordinary lives in the city's Black neighborhoods. "I wrote about what I saw and heard in the street," Brooks once said. "I lived in a small second-floor apartment at the corner, and I could look first on one side and then the other. There was my material." Brooks's Bronzeville neighborhood, once called the "Black Metropolis," was a thriving center of Black culture in the early nineteen hundreds as people migrated from the South in search of industrial jobs and to escape Jim Crow oppression.

In 1967 Brooks attended the Second Black Writer's Conference at Fisk University, and interaction there with young Black poets refocused her work. She made the decision to support independent Black publishers going forward, leaving Harper & Row. She also

---

* While we have seen both *Black* and *African American* named as acceptable terms, we have chosen to use *Black* in this book. This is both for consistency's sake and to honor the work of activists like Gwendolyn Brooks and the Black Lives Matter movement.

started a summer poetry workshop for the Blackstone Rangers, a group of young men and women from Chicago's South Side. Weekly meetings eventually moved to Brooks's home, where she would work with promising young poets, including Haki Madhubuti. Now a professor in his own right, Madhubuti rightly credits his teacher: "Her greatest lesson to us all is that serving one's community as an artist means much more than just creating art."

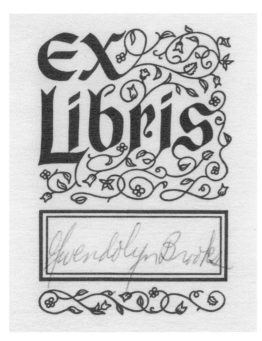

▲ Brooks was the author of more than twenty books of poetry, a novel, and an autobiography, as well as an editor of numerous poetry anthologies.

➤ Women gathered for an Easter parade in Chicago's Bronzeville neighborhood, circa 1941.

▲ As a testament to her legacy, many schools and libraries have been named after Brooks throughout Illinois.

rooks's service to community was evident throughout her life as a writer and teacher. While she worked in formal university settings around the country, her work was—and still is—an integral part of many writing and poetry curricula. As the Illinois poet laureate she made poetry accessible by bringing it to schools, prisons, and hospitals, as well as sponsoring children's writing contests and literary awards ceremonies. In her 1985–86 tenure as the consultant to poetry at the Library of Congress (now known as the poet laureate), she took an active role encouraging children in their own reading and writing. Brooks's daughter, Nora, is also a teacher and worked tirelessly to gather her mother's prolific archives, now accessible at the University of Illinois.

The notion of community is a critical aspect of Brooks's work. Her writing built upon—and contributed to—progress from the Harlem Renaissance to the civil rights movement. One challenge of using the term *community* is defining who is and is not included, something we recognize as privileged white women creating art about the Black community. Having grown up reading Brooks's poetry as a student in Detroit, then later as a Chicagoan, Jessica was eager to add her to our collection of dead feminists. Our decision to purposely include racist imagery felt like a real risk: do two white women have the right to tackle something so outside our own experience? Ultimately we saw it as worth the potential backlash, inspired in part by Brooks's own words and by some of the strong women of color that taught Jessica in grade school. We also felt the decision was made for us, when even cursory research about Black history unearthed a barrage of hateful imagery. Even as outsiders we still feel a connection to Brooks and all women—and a responsibility to counteract the racism we can

never unsee. After all Black Lives Matter was created by three Black women, Alicia Garza, Opal Tometi, and Patrisse Cullors, in response to the acquittal of George Zimmerman following the fatal shooting of Trayvon Martin, a Black teenager in Florida. While their methods are sometimes considered controversial and painted as militant by the media, their mission to "reimagine a world free from anti-Black racism, sexism, transmisogyny and economic disenfranchisement" encompasses a broader definition of community as our society moves forward. As always Brooks said it eloquently: "If we don't pull together, we won't be here to pull at all."

▲ Our donation went to 826CHI, a non-profit Chicago writing and tutoring center supporting students ages six to eighteen. Their mission is to "strengthen each student's power to express ideas effectively, creatively, confidently, and in his or her individual voice."

➤ Installed in 1996, Alison Saar's statue *Monument to the Great Northern Migration*, stands at the entrance to Bronzeville. Facing north, the traveler wears a suit made of worn shoe soles.

▲ In 1967 Organization of Black American Culture artists painted a mural on Chicago's South Side depicting Black heroes including Muhammad Ali, W. E. B. Du Bois, Malcolm X, Nina Simone, and Gwendolyn Brooks.

*1* Brooks was never one to pull a punch, so our broadside is an attempt to confront racism head-on.

*2* The illustration features a blood-red calico pattern of violence and cruelty, based on symbols of persistent cultural stereotypes.

*3* In tribute to the courage of those who fight for equality, the piece is a riot of color, glowing like an urban beacon.

*4* The typography here recalls the marquee of the famous Chicago Theatre.

*5* The graffiti overlays a stanza of Brooks's poem about the brutal 1955 murder of fourteen-year-old Emmett Till.

*6* To represent the glaring subtext behind so much of our culture, we printed our broadside in glowing fluorescent ink.

## "Reading is important. Read between the lines. Don't swallow everything."

## WARNING SIGNS

*No. 11 in the series*

**YEAR CREATED:** *2011*

**ISSUE:** *Persistent racism, violence, and stereotypes in American culture*

**EDITION:** *113 prints; Gwendolyn Brooks published her first poem at age thirteen*

**DONATION:** *826CHI*

# READING IS important READ BETWEEN the lines

## DON'T swallow EVERY-THING.

## Gwendolyn Brooks

Gwendolyn Tamika Elizabeth Brooks (1917 – 2000) grew up in Bronzeville, a neighborhood on Chicago's South Side where she "wrote about what I saw and heard on the street." Brooks published her first poem at age 13, and by 17 was a regular contributor to *Chicago Defender's* poetry column. Her first book, *A Street in Bronzeville*, was published in 1945, bringing critical acclaim and a Guggenheim Fellowship. In 1950 she became the first African American to win a Pulitzer Prize for her second book, *Annie Allen*. After attending a Black Writer's Conference at Fisk University in 1967, Brooks said she "rediscovered her blackness," reflected through *In The Mecca*, a book-length poem about a mother's search for her child lost in a Chicago housing project. Her work became leaner, more sharply focused, and she committed to publish only with independent African-American presses. Declaring "I want to write poems that will be non-compromising," Brooks continued to confront issues of race, gender and class.

As a teacher, poet laureate of Illinois and as poetry consultant to the Library of Congress, Brooks encouraged young poets through school visits and inner-city readings, bringing poetry to the people she spent her life writing about. She sponsored and hosted numerous literary awards, often with her own funds, committed to the idea that "poetry is life distilled."

Illustrated by Chandler O'Leary and printed by Jessica Spring, searching for clarity through a calico of misinformation, pernicious stereotypes and untold stories. 113 copies were printed by hand at Springtide Press in Tacoma. February 2011

CHANDLER O'LEARY          1/113

THEA
FOSS

ALICE
PAUL

ELEANOR
ROOSEVELT

# CHAPTER 2

These women planted seeds and cultivated growth. One sowed a Victory garden, but also grew herself into one of the most revered women in the twentieth century. Another nurtured a movement establishing a woman's right to vote. The last one tugged all the way to Hollywood, growing a business and a legend too.

GROW

# ELEANOR ROOSEVELT

Born Anna Eleanor Roosevelt on October 11, 1884, in New York City ✦ Wrote her syndicated My Day column six days a week from 1935 to 1962 ✦ Planted a White House Victory garden during World War II ✦ Served as the first chair of the UN Commission on Human Rights ✦ Died in 1962, buried at the family compound in Hyde Park

One of the most well-known and beloved women featured in our series, Eleanor Roosevelt (ER) grew into her role as First Lady of the World. After marrying her distant cousin Franklin Delano Roosevelt and having six children within eleven years, she described herself as "fitting pretty well into the pattern of a fairly conventional, quiet, young society matron." Things changed in 1918 as ER discovered FDR—in the midst of a burgeoning political career—was having an affair with her social secretary, Lucy Mercer. This event, plus the experience of attending the International Congress of Working Women and her work for the Red Cross, contributed to ER's shift in focus from "society matron" to political rabble-rouser.

When FDR contracted polio in 1921, ER nursed him back to health, encouraging his return to politics by her own involvement in the women's division of the State Democratic Committee. In 1928 FDR became governor of New York and ER was his trusted eyes and ears, going where he couldn't and reporting back. When he won the presidency in 1933, ER was reluctant to give up her busy, independent life, especially teaching history and government at the Todhunter School for Girls. Traditionally the role of first lady of the United States was that of housewife-in-chief—official hostess of state social events and promoter of "womanly" causes like children's welfare. ER found this expectation stifling, and desired a more active political career for herself.

When she came to the White House, ER quickly set a new standard for the modern first lady. She logged over forty thousand miles to investigate economic and social conditions, becoming an outspoken advocate for civil rights. She held 348 press conferences, the *first* first lady to do so, inviting only female reporters. In 1935 she began writing My Day, a syndicated newspaper column, often tackling controversial topics.

After FDR's death in 1945 ER was appointed by Truman to be the US delegate to the United Nations. Working tirelessly as chair of the United Nations Commission on Human Rights, she won passage of the Universal Declaration of Human Rights in 1948, which she considered her greatest achievement: "People grow through experience if they meet life honestly and courageously. This is how character is built."

▲ Not everyone appreciated ER's work as first lady; anti-Roosevelt campaigns targeted both FDR and his wife.

◄ Roosevelt and Mary McLeod Bethure, a member of FDR's Black Cabinet. Officially the Federal Council of Negro Affairs, it consisted of community leaders, activists, and political advisors strongly supported by ER.

▲ A five-cent commemorative stamp honoring Eleanor Roosevelt was issued October 11, 1963, on what would have been her seventy-ninth birthday. ER died of heart failure eleven months earlier.

► The Roosevelts with Anna and James in 1908. They had six children, although the first FDR Jr., born in 1909, died that same year. A second FDR Jr. was born in 1914.

**W**ar gardens or Victory gardens were promoted during both World War I and II to cultivate self-sufficiency and patriotism and were supported by progressives like Theodore Roosevelt. Women were called on to replace farmers sent to battle—these "farmerettes" were employed by the Women's Land Army of America and associated with the suffrage movement. In a show of support First Lady Edith Wilson brought a flock of sheep to graze on the White House lawn during World War I, and their wool was auctioned off to raise money for the Red Cross.

With the advent of rationing Victory gardens returned to popularity in World War II. In 1943, despite protests by the Department of Agriculture, ER planted a Victory garden at the White House. Inspired by the first lady's example, more than twenty million Americans had home gardens and participated in communal gardens from Golden Gate Park to Fenway (a garden in Boston that still operates today). This effort provided 40 percent of the country's fresh produce. Home canning was encouraged, both to preserve the abundance of foodstuffs and reduce the demand for tin.

Similarly inspired by ER, First Lady Michelle Obama broke ground on an 1,100-square-foot kitchen garden in March 2009. Her war garden was for a different sort of battle, though, fighting childhood obesity and sowing seeds for better nutrition. These issues, as well as ER's focus on self-sufficiency, inspire us to embrace homegrown and preserved foods and support local producers whenever possible.

➤ To augment their rations, it became a family's patriotic duty to plant a vegetable garden. Suddenly suburban housewives received a crash course in crop rotation and soil science.

# YOUR VICTORY GARDEN
## counts more than ever!

WAR FOOD ADMINISTRATION

◄ The US Office of War Information also employed the medium of the broadside, encouraging Americans to plant Victory gardens through a series of propaganda posters.

▼ During WWII the military reserved commodities for the troops. On the homefront everything from butter to silk stockings to gasoline was strictly rationed and women managed the use of household rations.

"We'll have lots to eat this winter, won't we Mother?"

Grow your own
Can your own

◄ The Victory garden effort didn't stop at planting and harvesting. The government also published pamphlets aimed at housewives, providing tips on how to prepare, store, and preserve homegrown goods.

*1* The orangerie at the Palace of Versailles inspired imagery for the White House lawn.

*2* The collection of metal type and ornaments (also called printer's flowers) at Springtide Press are a source Chandler often draws from.

*3* As private seed companies sought to profit from the Victory garden movement, each sought to outdo one another with their packaging.

*4* We also referenced the bold graphic shapes of World War II–era propaganda to sketch out our fantasy garden plot.

*5* Many of today's home gardeners stress the importance of organic food and seasonal eating as an impetus for changing the American agricultural system as a whole.

*6* Brocade comes from Italian *broccato* meaning embossed cloth. Found on upholstery and wallpaper at Versailles, brocades and velvets also inspired the lawn pattern.

*"The future belongs to those who believe in the beauty of their dreams."*

## VICTORY GARDEN

*No. 2 in the series*

**YEAR CREATED:** *2008*

**ISSUE:** *Return of the White House vegetable garden*

**EDITION:** *Seventy-six prints; Obama is the forty-fourth president and Franklin Roosevelt was the thirty-second, 44 + 32 = 76*

**DONATION:** *No donations made this early in the series*

THE **FUTURE** BELONGS TO THOSE WHO BELIEVE IN THE **BEAUTY** OF THEIR *dreams.*

ELEANOR ROOSEVELT

Anna Eleanor Roosevelt (1884–1962) transformed the role of first lady in the White House, where she served from 1933–45. In an effort to cultivate self-sufficiency and patriotism, she planted a Victory Garden on the White House lawn. Spurred in part by the first lady's example, more than 20 million Americans had home gardens and grew 40% of the country's produce during World War II. Today, amid rising food prices, climate change, and the finite supply of fossil fuels, we encourage the next first lady, Michelle Obama, to follow in Eleanor Roosevelt's footsteps and set an example for sustainability and hope once more — beginning on the White House lawn.

Illustrated by Chandler O'Leary and printed by Jessica Spring following the election of 2008. 76 copies were printed by hand at Springtide Press in Tacoma.

1/76

# ALICE PAUL

Born Alice Stokes Paul on January 11, 1885, in Moorestown,
New Jersey ✦ Imprisoned and force-fed while hunger striking in support of
women's suffrage ✦ Earned six degrees, including three in law that she used to
fight discrimination ✦ Wrote the original Equal Rights Amendment in 1923; to this
day it has yet to be enacted into law ✦ Debilitated by a stroke in 1974,
Paul died in 1977 in her hometown

Alice Paul spent her life with persistent, singular focus on growing the women's movement, attending her first suffrage meetings with her mother. Raised a Quaker (a faith founded on gender equality, with members notably involved in the woman's movement), she attended Swarthmore College and then took a one-year fellowship at a New York City settlement house. While pursuing her master's degree in London, she became active with the British suffrage movement. Paul joined in demonstrations, was arrested multiple times, and was forcibly fed while hunger striking in prison. She returned to the United States armed with militant experience and the motto: "Deeds, not words."

As a member of the National American Women's Suffrage Association (NAWSA), Paul was appointed to pursue federal suffrage. Staged to coincide with Woodrow Wilson's inauguration in 1913, Paul organized more than five thousand demonstrators to march up Pennsylvania Avenue. The event turned violent, as onlookers hurled insults and attacked the protesters while the police did nothing; as a result the movement was given national attention.

By 1916 Paul severed ties with NAWSA to form the National Woman's Party to focus solely on a national amendment—first for women's suffrage, then the Equal Rights Amendment. Directing their efforts at President Woodrow Wilson, members called "Silent Sentinels" would picket the White House six days a week. Wilson accused them of being unladylike, even unpatriotic to picket during wartime, but suffragists argued that if America could defend democracy abroad, they deserved it at home too. Despite their method of silent protest, the Sentinels were harassed, arrested, and then force-fed and assaulted in jail. Public outrage grew, the women were released, and Wilson finally announced support of the amendment in 1918. It took another year for the House and Senate to pass the Nineteenth Amendment giving women the right to vote, with the last state ratifying in 1920.

▲ Program cover for the 1913 parade led by lawyer and activist Inez Milholland, dressed in robes and riding a white stallion.

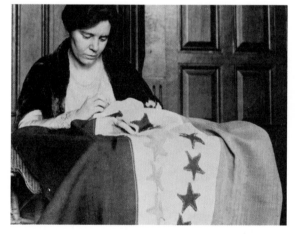

▲ The National Woman's Party created a suffrage flag, sewing on a star for each state that ratified the Nineteenth Amendment. Paul unfurled the flag at national headquarters after passage.

➤ Chairman Paul and National Woman's Party officers before leaving for the Chicago Convention to take the suffrage movement to the 1920 Republican Party Convention. Paul is second from the right.

ith Paul's leadership and the efforts of so many supporters, women finally had the right to vote. She then turned her efforts towards truly establishing "ordinary equality" by writing the Equal Rights Amendment: "Equality of rights under the law shall not be denied or abridged by the United States or by any state on account of sex." It passed in 1972—nearly fifty years after Paul first wrote it—but only thirty-five of the necessary thirty-eight states ratified the amendment, preventing it from being enacted into law. ERA opponents—notably right-wing leader Phyllis Schlafly and fundamentalist religious groups—used similar fear tactics employed by the anti-suffrage movement focusing on abortion and military service to ensure its failure. Despite ongoing efforts to pass the ERA, the only right currently guaranteed to women by federal law is the right to vote.

In November 2008 California voters approved Proposition 8, which declared "only marriage between a man and a woman is valid or recognized in California"—months after the state supreme court ruled same-sex marriages were legal. In response we used Paul's quote in support of the movement for marriage equality, in essence another demand for equal rights. Like the suffrage movement, marriage equality had been gaining traction but progress was dramatically halted by Prop 8. By 2012 it was ruled unconstitutional, and the movement grew state by state with the support of people of all genders and sexualities. It's as if Paul were describing the 2015 passage of marriage equality in all fifty states when she said: "The movement is a sort of mosaic. Each of us puts in one little stone, and then you get a great mosaic at the end."

As thrilling as this victory is, we need to continue moving forward to provide basic protections based on gender as well as gender identity and sexual orientation on a federal level.

➤ Photograph of Jimmy Carter signing the extension of the ERA ratification in 1978 as Rosalynn Carter looks on.

WHITE WINGS
WHEN THE SUFFRAGETTES GET CONTROL OF THE STREET-CLEANING DEPARTMENT.

▲ *Suffragette* was originally coined in the early twentieth century by the London *Daily Mail* as a pejorative label for suffragists. While some have reclaimed the term, it still remains controversial.

▲ To garner public support, suffragists employed symbols of American patriotism in their campaigns—like this replica of the Liberty Bell.

▼ The humble campaign button has a long tradition, as activists boiled their causes down to snappy slogans and memorable soundbites.

# TAKE A CLOSER LOOK AT *PROP CAKE*

*1* Chandler used San Francisco's iconic Painted Ladies—with their candy colors and frosting-like stucco—as inspiration.

*2* White paper beneath the ink-mixing glass gives us an idea of how the custom-mixed colors will look on each broadside.

*3* *Prop Cake* proved a challenge to print, requiring precise registration (line-up) of two colors, plus delicate line work and large floods.

*4* Suffrage sashes and banners were used as effective spectacles during marches and decorated with slogans.

*5* Chandler doesn't usually use special drawing tools, but since this broadside was influenced by architecture, she used several architect's tools.

*6* Despite changing times and matrimonial traditions, we referenced the towering wedding cakes and ornate confections of Paul's era.

## "There is nothing complicated about ordinary equality."

## PROP CAKE

*No. 3 in the series*

**YEAR CREATED:** *2009*

**ISSUE:** *Marriage equality and the passage of California Proposition 8*

**EDITION:** *108 prints; the eight represents Proposition 8*

**DONATION:** *No donations made this early in the series*

ALICE PAUL

THERE·IS

NOTHING

COMPLICATED

ABOUT ordinary

EQUALITY.

Alice Stokes Paul (1885 – 1977) continued the work of the suffragists, and helped form the National Woman's Party to demand equal rights. The NWP engaged in militant demonstrations and the first picketing of the White House; these "Silent Sentinels" were mobbed and imprisoned, then force-fed while attempting a hunger strike. Public and media support for their cause grew and by 1920, women secured the vote. Alice Paul continued to work on their behalf, writing the original Equal Rights Amendment in 1923. ILLUSTRATED BY CHANDLER O'LEARY AND PRINTED BY JESSICA SPRING, WHO THINK EVERYONE DESERVES AN EQUAL SLICE OF WEDDING CAKE. 108 COPIES WERE PRINTED BY HAND AT SPRINGTIDE PRESS IN TACOMA. FEBRUARY 2009.

CHANDLER O'LEARY                    5/108

# THEA FOSS

Born Thea Christiansen (née Christiansdatter) on June 8, 1857, in Eidsberg, Ostfold, Norway ✦ Helped found Daughters of Norway Lodge #2 in Tacoma in 1908, and served as secretary ✦ Founded Foss Maritime, which still operates one of the West Coast's largest fleets of tugboats and is part of an international marine services network ✦ Died in 1927, just a few days before her sixty-ninth birthday

Recently emigrated and newly married in 1889, Thea Foss set down roots—or at least an anchor—in a floating home on the waterfront in Tacoma, Washington. While her husband, Andrew, worked in the valley as a carpenter, Foss bought a used rowboat for five dollars from an unsuccessful fisherman. With some green and white paint, she fixed it up and sold it for fifteen dollars. She bought a few more boats and then began renting them for fifty cents a day. By the time Andrew returned home she had earned forty-one dollars—more than he had made building sheds—and launched a thriving business.

By the early nineteen hundreds the Foss Launch Company employed the whole Foss family, relatives from Norway as well as other Scandinavian immigrants. In addition to her children, Foss took responsibility for a boarding house, a company store, and offices while regularly cooking and counseling a large crew of employees who called Foss and her husband Mother and Father Foss. Her charity work at the Norwegian Church often focused on young immigrant girls, and she made their home a welcoming place for the community.

Foss's life loosely inspired a series of stories written for the *Saturday Evening Post* by Norman Reilly Raine. The main character, Tugboat Annie, is a tough little skipper from Secoma (Seattle plus Tacoma). The stories—more than sixty were published from the 1930s to the 1960s—pit Annie against male chauvinists who think "that managing a towing and salvage company is a man's job." Time and again she proves them wrong, overcoming nasty tricks with quick thinking and a forceful personality, providing laughs along the way.

While Foss's legend lives on through the character of Tugboat Annie, her real legacy survives her in Tacoma, Washington. Foss Maritime tugs are still painted green and white, bearing family names, and Tacoma's working waterfront is called the Thea Foss Waterway. Her namesake park has a plaque that shares her approach to a life well-grown: "The whole world is my family."

▲ The Foss boathouse became a fixture along the Tacoma waterfront.

▲ This two-color cut of the Foss logo was recovered from a commercial print shop that was founded in Tacoma over a century ago.

▶ Lobby card from the 1933 MGM film *Tugboat Annie*, starring Marie Dressler and Wallace Beery.

**F**oss's story is amazing, but even more so considering when it happened. In 1889 the majority of women in the workforce were single and typically employed as teachers, nurses, postmistresses, milliners, factory workers in mills and canneries, and even artists and performers. Many married women supplemented their family income with piecework and domestic chores, but stay-at-home motherhood was the ideal. With the turn of the century, the suffrage movement, and bloomers and bicycles for women, progress finally caught up to Foss.

Our call to action on her print refers to an old saying: "Man may work from sun to sun, but woman's work is never done." In a culture where "work" must generate income or produce goods, we continue to undervalue the critical contributions of whoever does the unpaid, undervalued work at home. This is still predominantly women, and they are doing this work in addition to comprising more than half the workforce today. Add to that dramatic gender- and race-based wage gaps despite equal levels of education and experience, and the inequities still feel like corsets and bustles. Parity is not just a woman's issue: demand equality and we *all* benefit. Foss knew this a long, long time ago: "We are members of one great body, and we must consider we were born for the good of the whole."

▲ ➤ The Industrial Revolution ushered in a new era of tradeswomen—including our foremothers in printing and typesetting.

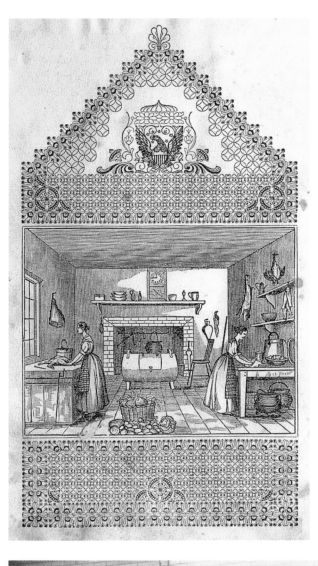

◄ From *The New England Economical House-keeper and Family Receipt Book*. "Home economics" is often associated with housewives, but at the turn of the twentieth century, it was an accepted formal field of study.

▼ Like Foss Scandinavian immigrant women would gather with their children to enjoy coffee, conversation, and handcrafts.

▲ Nearly nineteen million women held jobs during World War II, often nontraditional and higher paying work, but were expected to return home once the war ended.

# TAKE A CLOSER LOOK AT *TUGBOAT THEA*

**1** Our first Foss print was actually a huge linoleum carving printed with a steamroller at a local letterpress festival.

**2** Filmmaker Nancy Bourne Haley inspired us to turn the print into a broadside with a quote from her *Finding Thea* documentary.

**3** A ship's figurehead—often carved as a woman—provides luck and safe passage. Foss successfully guided her business through choppy waters.

**4** Foss's business flourished in Puget Sound, home to the giant Pacific octopus as shown here in the process of inking.

**5** Foss leased a tugboat to MGM for the 1934 movie *Tugboat Annie*. Rechristened the *Arthur Foss*, it's moored in Seattle.

**6** We chose a marine color scheme that evokes the signature Foss green and white, plus a silvery gray evocative of Puget Sound waters.

## "*There are so many things left to do.*"

## TUGBOAT THEA

*No. 4 in the series*

**YEAR CREATED:** *2009*

**ISSUE:** *Women's entrepreneurship*

**EDITION:** *Eighty-nine prints; Washington gained statehood and Thea Foss opened her business in 1889*

**DONATION:** *No donations made this early in the series*

# THERE ARE SO MANY THINGS Left to do

THEA FOSS

Norwegian immigrant Thea Christiansen Foss (1857 – 1927) arrived by train to Tacoma in 1889 as Washington achieved statehood. While her husband Andrew was at work she spent five dollars on a rowboat, launching a marine transport business that would grow into Foss Maritime, operating the west coast's largest fleet of tugboats. Thea inspired the character "Tugboat Annie" featured in a *Saturday Evening Post* series, motion pictures and a television show. Tacoma's Thea Foss Waterway is an inlet connected to Puget Sound named in her honor.

Illustrated by Chandler O'Leary and printed by Jessica Spring in recognition that a woman's work is never done. 89 copies were printed by hand at Springtide Press — not far from the water — in Tacoma. May 2009.

Chandler O'Leary                              2/89                              Jessica Spring

ANNIE
OAKLEY

ADINA
DE ZAVALA

RACHEL
CARSON

# CHAPTER 3

# PROTECT

While women have traditionally been seen as protectors, especially in their parenting roles, these dead feminists took on some big issues outside the family. One taught women the importance of gun safety, another secured a national symbol, while another focused attention on environmental dangers.

# ANNIE OAKLEY

Born Phoebe Ann Mosey (or Moses) on August 13, 1860, near Greenville, Ohio ✦ Met husband Frank Butler in 1875 by defeating him in a shooting contest ✦ Performed with Buffalo Bill's Wild West show for seventeen years ✦ Was the first cowgirl ever to appear in a motion picture ✦ Died in 1926, just days before Butler's death

Annie Oakley lived at time before feminism had a name, yet she came to embody both feminist ideals and the spirit of the American West. She defined our notion of a cowgirl as being strong, self-reliant, resourceful, and highly skilled. She was self-made in every way, and built her life and career on her own terms.

Oakley was born to a family of Quaker farmers in 1860, near Greenville, Ohio. After she lost her father at a young age, she taught herself to shoot a rifle and quickly paid off the family mortgage by selling game. At the age of just fifteen, Oakley defeated well-known marksman Frank Butler in a shooting contest—and married him a year later. She became his assistant in his sharpshooting show, but it didn't take long for Butler to notice that audiences clearly preferred his wife. He suggested they switch roles, and he became *her* assistant instead. The act that would become their trademark was born, and Annie Oakley became both headliner and breadwinner.

Oakley and Butler joined Buffalo Bill Cody's Wild West show in 1885, where they performed internationally for seventeen years. Upon seeing her shoot the wick off a burning candle, the famous Chief Sitting Bull adopted Oakley as his daughter and a member of the Hunkpapa Lakota tribe, bestowing upon her the nickname "Watanya Cicilla" (Lakota for Little Sure-Shot). In 1894 Thomas Edison captured her performance on film at his New Jersey studio, making her the first cowgirl to appear in a motion picture. She continued to set shooting records into her sixties, and through it all, she remained devoted to Butler. After fifty years of marriage, they both passed away in 1926, within days of one another.

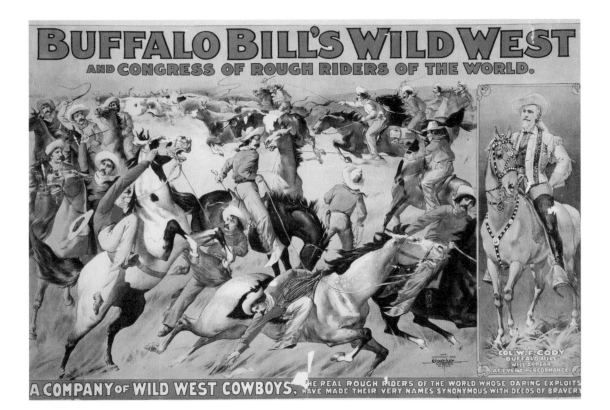

BUFFALO BILL'S WILD WEST
AND CONGRESS OF ROUGH RIDERS OF THE WORLD.

COL. W. F. CODY
BUFFALO BILL
WILL APPEAR
AT EVERY PERFORMANCE

A COMPANY OF WILD WEST COWBOYS, THE REAL ROUGH RIDERS OF THE WORLD WHOSE DARING EXPLOITS HAVE MADE THEIR VERY NAMES SYNONYMOUS WITH DEEDS OF BRAVERY

▲ Oakley and Butler had a marriage that was ahead of its time. Oakley was the primary breadwinner from the time she was a teenager, while Butler supported her career.

◄ Oakley performed several signature tricks, including shooting over her shoulder while aiming with a mirror. Her most famous feat was to split a playing card edge-on from ninety feet, using a .22 caliber rifle.

oth Oakley's onstage persona and her personal life helped pave the way for modern feminism—reinforcing her role as a protector. She was an advocate of equal pay for women—at the peak of her career, she was the second highest-paid performer in the Wild West show, behind only Bill Cody himself. She was also a philanthropist for women's rights, quietly donating money throughout her life to causes that supported women. She spent her retirement teaching over fifteen thousand women to use firearms responsibly, believing strongly that every woman should learn to protect herself and her family.

Oakley's faith in self-defense and protection extended to her own life as well. When William Randolph Hearst published a libelous story about her in his national newspapers, Oakley spent over six years defending her reputation in court. She won fifty-four of fifty-five libel lawsuits against the Hearst newspaper empire, all at her own expense. Oakley's strong convictions—and her willingness to protect them—made her a feminist pioneer.

Oakley's stance on firearms and her work as a protector provide plenty of food for thought in the wake of seemingly endless mass-shooting tragedies in America. While we don't personally support gun ownership ourselves, we recognize that firearms are a deeply ingrained part of American culture. At the same time we wish to protect ourselves and others from violence. In that spirit we donated a portion of our proceeds to Demand a Plan. A campaign of Mayors Against Illegal Guns, Demand a Plan is a national, bipartisan coalition working to protect American communities by keeping illegal guns out of dangerous hands.

▲ Oakley felt it was important for every woman to be able to protect herself and her family. She spent her life after retirement traveling the country teaching women to shoot.

▲ A rally on the steps of the US Capitol on "Gun Safety Day" organized by the US Conference of Mayors in 1999.

◄ Oakley's defense of gun ownership was different from the modern rhetoric of the NRA; her world of marksmanship competitions is a far cry from civilian access to semiautomatic assault rifles.

▲ Our biggest challenge was depicting the middle ground—represented by the golden bullseye of sanity, amid the scatter-shot opinions and half-cocked sniping of those on the extremist fringes.

*1* Oakley rejected the skimpy outfits she was asked to wear on stage and made her own costumes.

*2* We referenced vintage shooting targets in the design of our giant bullseye.

*3* Oakley proudly wore her numerous sharpshooting medals as part of her costume.

*4* The hand-lettered text of our broadside is a nod to the American Wild West.

*5* The somber color scheme is punctuated with metallic ink infused with real gold powder.

*6* Our portrait is inspired by Oakley's many publicity photos, which depict her as a symbol of strength and femininity: the quintessential cowgirl.

*"Aim at a high mark, work for the future."*

## GUN SHY

*No. 17 in the series*

**YEAR CREATED:** *2013*

**ISSUE:** *Gun control*

**EDITION:** *151 prints; number of people killed or injured in shooting rampages in 2012*

**DONATION:** *Demand a Plan*

# AIM AT A HIGH MARK

## Annie Oakley

**WORK FOR THE FUTURE**

7 8 9 8 9 8 7

★ LITTLE ★ SURE ★ SHOT ★

Annie Oakley (1860–1926) was born Phoebe Ann Mosey (or Moses) near Greenville, Ohio. Her Quaker parents raised seven children on their farm until Annie's father was caught in a blizzard and succumbed to pneumonia. By age ten, Annie was sent to the poor farm, then to live with an abusive family for several years. She escaped back to her mother's home, taught herself to shoot a rifle, and quickly paid off their mortgage by selling game. In 1875 Annie defeated well-known marksman Frank Butler in a shooting contest — and married him shortly afterward. Annie became Butler's assistant in his sharp shooting show, but as audiences clearly preferred Annie, the two soon switched roles. Annie was a curiosity, dressed in a homemade costume that modestly covered her petite frame but also allowed her to shoot with athletic grace. The couple joined Buffalo Bill Cody's Wild West show, where Annie performed for 17 years, traveling to New York, Paris and London. Upon seeing her shoot the wick off a burning candle, the famous Chief Sitting Bull adopted Annie, bestowing the nickname "Watanya Cicilla" (Little Sure-Shot). In 1894 Thomas Edison captured her performance on film at his studio in New Jersey, making her the first cowgirl to appear in a motion picture.

Despite not being from the West, Annie defined our notion of a cowgirl as a self-reliant, strong woman. She advocated for equal pay, and went to great lengths to defend her reputation. She challenged William Randolph Hearst in a series of libel lawsuits over a false newspaper story, winning 54 of 55 cases at great personal expense. After her retirement in 1913, Annie continued to tour the country, teaching over 15,000 women how to use firearms responsibly.

Illustrated by Chandler O'Leary and printed by Jessica Spring, demanding that our federal government enact strict controls to end gun violence. 151 copies were printed by hand at Springtide Press in Tacoma. February 2013

Chandler O'Leary                    79/151

# ADINA DE ZAVALA

Born Adina Emilia De Zavala on November 28, 1861, in Harris County, Texas ✦ Founded the Daughters of the Republic of Texas (DRT) ✦ Saved the iconic Alamo from demolition by camping inside the ruined building ✦ Died in 1955, successful in her preservation efforts

Adina De Zavala was another protector—though of a very different sort. She devoted her life to the protection of historic property, and the preservation of her city for all to explore and enjoy.

De Zavala was born in 1861, the granddaughter of the first vice president of the Republic of Texas. As a young adult in San Antonio, De Zavala worked as a teacher, bringing her Tejana heritage and her love of Texas history to her students. In her spare time she solicited donations of building supplies to repair the city's Spanish missions. Inspired by her grandfather's history, De Zavala helped found the Daughters of the Republic of Texas (DRT) to preserve Mission San Antonio de Valero—better known as the Alamo.

De Zavala was especially focused on restoring the mission's barracks. Many people supported their demolition, but De Zavala's research—including interviews with soldiers' families—proved the barracks were part of the 1836 Battle of the Alamo. For Texans the Battle of the Alamo was a defining historical moment where for thirteen days the defenders, vastly outnumbered, held the fort against Mexican forces, and inspired their continued struggle for independence. In 1905, days before the Alamo lease would expire, as rumors spread of imminent conversion to a hotel, De Zavala locked herself in the rat-infested structure without food, demanding that the entire compound be preserved. "If people—especially children—can actually see the door through which some noble man or woman passed," she said, "they'll be impressed; they'll remember." After three days, she was released as the governor took possession, and then returned control to the DRT. Thanks to De Zavala's persistence and the DRT's ongoing stewardship, the legendary Alamo is preserved as a museum, state shrine, and national historic landmark, open to all people to visit, free of charge.

▲ Originally called Mission San Antonio de Valero, the Alamo was built in 1718 by the Spanish to evangelize Indigenous peoples. It later housed the Mexican army.

▶ The Alamo has been a central figure in the history of Texas and Mexico. Today, thanks to De Zavala and the DRT, the mission and grounds are preserved.

▼ After the Battle of the Alamo, the Republic of Texas returned the shrine to the Catholic Church. When Texas was annexed in 1845, the complex began to fall into disrepair.

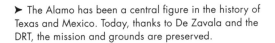

For our ninth broadside, *On a Mission*, we featured a quote by De Zavala that included the words *hold the fort*—a phrase we had heard before in a very different context. At the time we were creating the piece, the state of Arizona had just passed a controversial and sweeping immigration reform bill called SB1070. It was the broadest and strictest immigration bill that had ever been passed, and we believed it encouraged racial profiling. We kept hearing the phrase *hold the fort* used against Latino immigrants, with demands to strengthen US borders, and even in threats to build huge fences. Since De Zavala believed in preserving Texas history and the symbolism of the Alamo for *everyone*, we wanted to reclaim the phrase in a positive way, respecting her work as a preservationist and honoring the important contributions of immigrants.

*On a Mission* is filled with imagery and references to the cultural diversity of the American Southwest. With our design, we hoped to capture the spirit of De Zavala's fight to save the Alamo by extending the ideal of inclusivity to the battle against racial profiling.

▲ De Zavala helped save one historic structure, but preservationists fight an uphill battle to continue to protect the cultural and natural wonders of the Southwest, like Mesa Verde.

PACKING UP.

▲ The Pacific Northwest has also suffered anti-immigration sentiment, both past and present. We donated to the Northwest Immigrant Rights Project, which promotes the legal rights of immigrants and refugees.

◄ What we think of as the "American" Southwest is iconic and dear to us because of the peoples with whom we share it. To celebrate this our broadside references Central American folk art.

# TAKE A CLOSER LOOK AT *ON A MISSION*

*1* Our design begins with an homage to the famous landscapes of the American Southwest.

*2* Blackletter typefaces are used commonly in Mexico for signage, and are prevalent in graffiti created by Mexican-American artists.

*3* Both Mexican and Navajo silverwork is part of the heritage of the Southwest.

*4* Hidden in our design is the famous silhouette of the Alamo.

*5* To illustrate the thorny problem of immigration reform, we filled our design with images of native Southwest cacti.

*6* Our design is festooned with *milagros* (Spanish for "miracles")— religious votives that adorn church walls in thanks for blessings received.

*"There was nothing else for me to do but hold the fort. So I did."*

## ON A MISSION

*No. 9 in the series*

**YEAR CREATED:** *2010*

**ISSUE:** *Arizona immigration reform bill (SB1070)*

**EDITION:** *175 prints; number of years (at the time of printing) since the Battle of the Alamo*

**DONATION:** *Northwest Immigrant Rights Project*

THERE WAS NOTHING ELSE for me TO·DO BUT

HOLD the FORT.

SO I DID.

As a young Tejana teacher, Adina Emilia De Zavala (1861 – 1955) shared her love of Texas history and legends in her classroom, and spent time outside of school soliciting building supplies to repair San Antonio's missions. In honor of her Mexican grandfather, the Republic's first Vice President, she founded the Daughters of the Republic of Texas (DRT) in order to preserve the Mission San Antonio de Valero. The compound was built in 1718 by the Spanish to evangelize local Native Americans, then later — as the Alamo — housed the Mexican Army. De Zavala was especially focused on restoring the long barracks, which she believed was the site of the 1836 Battle of the Alamo. In 1905, days before the Alamo lease would expire and rumors spread of imminent conversion to a hotel, De Zavala locked herself in the rat-infested structure without food, demanding that the entire compound be preserved. "If people – especially children – can actually see the door through which some noble man or woman passed," she said "they'll be impressed; they'll remember." After three days, De Zavala was released as the Governor took possession, then returned control to the DRT. Thanks to De Zavala's persistence and the DRT's ongoing stewardship, the legendary Alamo is preserved as a museum and National Historic Landmark, open to all people.

Illustrated by Chandler O'Leary and printed by Jessica Spring, as thorny issues arise and tear at our shared history and heritage: a multicultural miracle that demands tolerance even in the most trying times. 175 copies were printed by hand, with heart, at Springtide Press in Tacoma. August 2010

CHANDLER O'LEARY                    38/175

# RACHEL CARSON

Born Rachel Louise Carson on May 27, 1907, in Springdale, Pennsylvania ✦ Published her first story at age ten, beginning a writing career focused on the natural world ✦ Worked as a marine biologist for the US Fish and Wildlife Service ✦ Wrote *Silent Spring*, a groundbreaking and controversial book on the effects of pesticides ✦ Died in 1964; her work led to the creation of the US Environmental Protection Agency

Rachel Louise Carson devoted her life to the protection of the environment—first as a scientist and later as a best-selling author and shaper of government policy.

The natural world was Carson's biggest influence from the beginning. Born in 1907 on a small family farm overlooking Pennsylvania's Allegheny River, Carson spent her early years exploring the woods and reading the books of Beatrix Potter. She wrote (and published) animal stories as a child, and studied biology in college. After earning a master's degree in zoology from Johns Hopkins University, she went to work for the US Bureau of Fisheries (later renamed the Fish and Wildlife Service). Her job required her to write about marine life for the general public; her ability to make science accessible to laypersons led to a career writing for major magazines and publishers. Her experience as a marine biologist and essayist laid the groundwork for a "sea trilogy" where science meets prose: *Under the Sea Wind* (1941), *The Sea Around Us* (1950), and *The Edge of the Sea* (1955).

Carson's later career focused on conservation and centered on the detrimental effects of chemical pesticides. Her most famous book, *Silent Spring* (1962), focused on dichlorodiphenyltrichloroethane (DDT) and its effects on bird species. The book's careful research and popularity as an international best seller led to the eventual ban of DDT nationwide, despite heavy opposition from the chemical industry. Her work inspired the modern environmental movement, paving the way towards the formation of the US Environmental Protection Agency and the passage of the Endangered Species Act. Carson was memorialized with a posthumous Presidential Medal of Freedom and a national wildlife refuge in coastal Maine that bears her name.

▲ Carson worked in the field with wildlife artist Robert Hines, who was also employed by the US Bureau of Fisheries.

"I USE BISON
DIDIT
IT REALLY DOES
KILL"

THE LADIES KNOW WHAT'S GOOD!

Across the continent, housewives quickly discovered Bison DIDIT to be a new and better killer of disease carrying flies, mosquitoes, bedbugs and roaches...protection against hateful moths...good riddance to most household insect pests.

Bison DIDIT, America's proven insecticide licensed under a U.S. Patent to contain 5% Technical Grade of the amazing wartime chemical DDT, is simple to use...no muss...just spray this sure death to most household insect pests. The pleasant, mild odor when spraying quickly disappears, And Bison DIDIT leaves no stains...just an invisible residual toxicity that can continue to kill for days.

THE PROVEN, KILLING SPRAY
BISON
DIDIT
Contains 5% Technical Grade DDT
INSECT SPRAY
KILLS FLIES, MOTHS, FLEAS, ROACHES MOSQUITOES, ANTS, BED BUGS
Guaranteed by
Good Housekeeping

"AND LOOK"
Your favorite magazine has found Bison DIDIT to be good...good enough to carry Good Housekeeping's guarantee. Yours is good judgment when you ask for Bison DIDIT Insect Spray wherever you shop.

Guaranteed by
Good Housekeeping

**BISON LABORATORIES · BUFFALO 11, N. Y.**

▲ DDT was first used during WWII to combat malaria and typhus. After the war the chemical was widely used as an agricultural pesticide—until Carson exposed its devastating effects.

◄ Eggshell thinning caused by DDT decimated bird populations, particularly the brown pelican and birds of prey like the bald eagle and peregrine falcon.

O n April 20, 2010, the offshore oil rig known as the Deepwater Horizon exploded and sank, resulting in the largest marine oil spill in the history of petroleum extraction. An estimated 210 million gallons of oil poured into the Gulf of Mexico, first from the damaged well that gushed for eighty-seven days, and then from leaks that continued to flow from improper sealing of the wellhead. Oil, tar balls, byproducts, and toxins continued to wash ashore from Louisiana to Tampa Bay as late as 2013, and ongoing effects to the Gulf ecosystem are still being measured and studied.

Carson would have been horrified by the size and scope of the Deepwater Horizon disaster. The area affected by the spill is home to over eight thousand species of fish, mollusks, reptiles, birds, and mammals—all of which are part of a complex and delicate food chain. In light of the staggering number of species affected by the spill, our *Drill, Baby, Drill* broadside focuses on the diversity of Gulf wildlife. The design is teeming with life—walking, flying, perching, floating, nesting, crawling, and swimming over the quote, which flows through the piece like the lines of a poem. In the end Carson's words give us hope that one day the Gulf will recover: "Those who contemplate the beauty of the earth find reserves of strength that will endure as long as life lasts."

▲ Carson took her fight over DDT to the government, testifying before Congress on the effects of pesticides.

▲ The 2010 Deepwater Horizon oil spill still wreaks havoc on the Gulf of Mexico. Oil slicks line the sea floor, methane has created "dead zones" devoid of life, and the food chain has been affected with mutations.

▲ Pictured is the Rachel Carson Wildlife Refuge in Maine. In honor of Carson's work to protect wildlife, we made a donation to Oceana, an international nonprofit dedicated to ocean conservation.

▶ In 1949 Carson visited the Florida Everglades, inspiring her book *The Sea Around Us*. Dozens of mammal species, hundreds of bird varieties, and thousands of types of fish and crustaceans have been affected by oil spills.

# TAKE A CLOSER LOOK AT *DRILL, BABY, DRILL*

**1** The broadside is printed in ocean blue, as well as a tawny gold representing both Gulf sand and the sickly tea color of spilled crude oil.

**2** The title of the piece, *Drill, Baby, Drill*, is a reference to a campaign slogan used by pro-oil Republican politicians like Sarah Palin.

**3** The muted palette is accented with hand-painted pink, to call out vibrant species like the roseate spoonbill and Gulf shrimp.

**4** Just as Carson's long-form quote is overflowing with words and imagery, our design is brimming with diverse animal species.

**5** The brown pelican was extremely vulnerable to DDT. Populations recovering since the ban were severely affected by the Gulf oil spill.

**6** People flocked to buy *Drill, Baby, Drill*, our most popular broadside to date. The edition sold out in twenty-four hours.

"*To stand at the edge of the sea, to feel the ebb and flow of the tides, to feel the breath of a mist moving over a great salt marsh, to watch the flight of shorebirds that have swept up and down the sun lines of the continents for untold thousands of year . . . is to have knowledge of things that are as nearly eternal as any earthly life can be.*"

## DRILL, BABY, DRILL

*No. 8 in the series*

**YEAR CREATED:** *2010*

**ISSUE:** *Offshore oil drilling and the Deepwater Horizon oil spill*

**EDITION:** *136 prints; thirty-six years (at the time of printing) since the passage of the Endangered Species Act*

**DONATION:** *Oceana*

to Stand at the EDGE of the SEA, to sense the EBB and FLOW of the tides, to Feel the Breath of a Mist MOVING OVER A GREAT SALT MARSH, TO WATCH THE FLIGHT of SHORE BIRDS that have swept up and down THE SUN LINES of the CONTINENTS FOR UNTOLD THOUSANDS OF YEAR... IS TO HAVE Knowledge OF THINGS THAT ARE AS NEARLY ETERNAL AS ANY EARTHLY LIFE CAN BE.

Rachel Louise Carson (1907 – 1964) was born in rural Pennsylvania, where she was "happiest with wild birds and creatures as companions." After majoring in science in college, Rachel won a fellowship at the Marine Biological Laboratory at Woods Hole and pursued marine zoology at Johns Hopkins. Carson had a long career with the US Fish and Wildlife Service and wrote numerous books and articles, including *Under the Sea-Wind, The Sea Around Us, The Sense of Wonder,* and the best-seller *Silent Spring,* in which she warned an uninformed public about the dangerous overuse of chemicals like DDT. The book— reminding us of our critical part in nature and the potential to cause irreversible harm—

launched the environmental movement that led to the formation of the Environmental Protection Agency and the passage of the Endangered Species Act. Carson is memorialized with a National Wildlife Refuge in her name and a posthumous Presidential Medal of Freedom.

Illustrated by Chandler O'Leary and printed by Jessica Spring, as oil pours into the Gulf Coast, leaving tar balls on the beaches and moving inland towards salt marshes. 136 copies were printed by hand at Springtide Press in Tacoma. June 2010

RACHEL · CARSON

CHANDLER O'LEARY          49/136

IMOGEN CUNNINGHAM

SADAKO SASAKI

ELIZABETH ZIMMERMANN

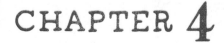

# CHAPTER 4

# Make

Throughout human history, women have assumed the role of makers. As artists, craftswomen, hobbyists, and homemakers, women have used their hands to shape and influence the world around them. The dead feminists in this chapter were extraordinary makers, remembered chiefly for their creations—which survive to this day as their legacies.

# Imogen Cunningham

Born April 12, 1883, in Portland, Oregon ✦ Graduated from the University of Washington with a degree in chemistry ✦ After college, worked for famed Seattle photographer Edward S. Curtis ✦ Focused on portraiture and botanicals in her own photographic work ✦ Died in 1976, after a career that spanned nearly seventy years

Imogen Cunningham was a prolific artist and a pioneer of photography, leaving behind many hundreds of images captured by her eye and lens. As a living mirror of the world around her, she was a maker of the highest caliber.

Cunningham hailed from the Pacific Northwest—born in 1883 in Portland, Oregon, she grew up in Seattle and attended college at the University of Washington. There she earned a degree in chemistry, writing her thesis on darkroom chemicals and photographic chemistry. After graduating she went to work for Edward S. Curtis, a well-known Seattle photographer who taught her the ins and outs of running a portrait business. She later moved to Oakland, California, and applied her knowledge to a long run in professional por-traiture, shooting celebrity photos for the magazine *Vanity Fair*. Cunningham's work led her to meet other important photographers of the day, and she helped found Group f/64 that included seven artists interested in a modernist approach to photography.

While running her one-woman business as a portrait photographer, Cunningham used her spare time to develop her more artistic work. She was perhaps best known for her dramatic black-and-white photographs of nudes and botan-ical forms. The crisp focus, sharp contrast, and abstract shapes of Cunningham's plants and figures make them some of the most iconic photographs of the twentieth century.

▶ Two subjects to which Cunningham returned again and again were nude figures and botanical forms. While studying at the University of Washington, she processed slides for botanists at the campus lab.

▼ Cunningham spent a few years as a portrait photographer for *Vanity Fair*, capturing celebrities of the day. Frida Kahlo, Cary Grant, and Martha Graham were some of her most famous subjects.

▲ It's important for artists to hone their skills as observers and image makers. Chandler attends sketch sessions with live models to keep her seeing eye sharp and her drawing hand confident.

s makers ourselves we recognize the power of observation and the artist's eye. So Cunningham's words have a special resonance with us. Yet we know all too well that the world is full of distractions, and it is far easier to move through life without stopping to observe, process, and capture one's surroundings. Cunningham didn't let that happen. She found beauty and drama all around her in the simple lines and shadows of everyday objects and people. And she kept creating new work, no matter what, as evidenced by her words: "I never stopped photographing. There were a couple of years when I didn't have a darkroom, but that didn't stop me from photographing." Cunningham built a life and career out of what she saw, and left a lasting legacy of images behind her.

It takes years of training and practice to hone one's abilities as an image maker. It's one thing to have a "seeing eye"—it's another thing entirely to really *look* at one's surroundings, and use one's sight to make a statement. Not everyone has automatic access to this kind of learning, so it was important to us to make an impact for the next generation of artists and photographers. Even for those who don't seek a career in the arts, creating images can be a fulfilling lifelong hobby. With that goal in sight, we donated a portion of our proceeds to the Seattle nonprofit Youth in Focus. To develop the seeing eyes of at-risk urban teens, Youth in Focus puts cameras in their hands and teaches them the art of photography. We admire the photography-centered mission of the organization, and their commitment to using cameras to teach teens "how to develop negatives into positives."

▲ Photography can be an expensive career or pastime. By donating to Youth in Focus, we hoped to give teens access to an art form that might otherwise be out of reach.

▲ Well before the advent of digital photography and social-media selfies, hobby photographers were taking advantage of high-tech tools and equipment.

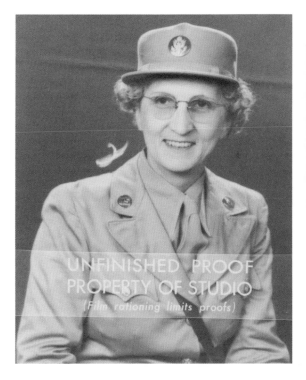

▲ Women often take on the role of documentarians within their own families, preserving events and memories in photo albums and scrapbooks.

◄ Photo-developing chemicals were heavily rationed during World War II. For everyone from home hobbyists to professionals like Cunningham, darkroom supplies were a precious commodity during the war.

**1** This is our first broadside ever printed on black paper, an homage to Cunningham's dedication to black-and-white images.

**2** Surrounding the quote is an intricate metallic silver filigree of botanicals and portraiture—a pastiche of Cunningham's most iconic subjects.

**3** The tangled plantlife depicted in *Focal Point* references Cunningham's exploration of botanical images.

**4** In the eye of the storm of imagery is the all-seeing camera lens, looking out onto the world.

**5** The style of imagery is reminiscent of Jessica's library of vintage metal image cuts—an early predecessor of modern clip art.

**6** We had to keep our "seeing eyes" in sharp focus when we printed: black paper and metallic ink emphasized any small printing flaws.

## "The seeing eye is the important thing."

## FOCAL POINT

*No. 19 in the series*

**YEAR CREATED:** *2014*

**ISSUE:** *The unique vision of artists; staying focused in a world full of distractions*

**EDITION:** *164 prints; the photography collective co-founded by Cunningham is called Group f/64*

**DONATION:** *Youth in Focus*

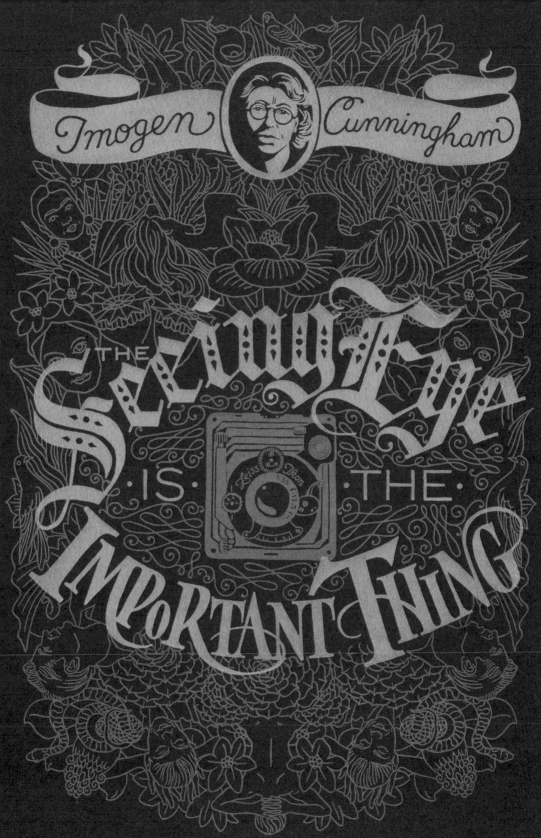

# Imogen Cunningham

## The Seeing Eye ·is· the· Important Thing

Imogen Cunningham (1883 – 1976) graduated from the University of Washington in 1907, earning a degree in chemistry with her thesis on chemical processes in photography. Shortly afterward she was hired by photographer Edward Curtis, who taught her platinum printing and portraiture. She opened her own successful studio in Seattle, and published an article entitled "Photography as a Profession for Women." In 1917, Cunningham and her husband and son relocated to California, where she gave birth to twin boys. Her children and the plants in her garden then became key subjects of her work. Her experiments with double exposure throughout the 1920s and 30s contributed to a growing appreciation of photography as art. She was a founding member of Group f/64, a collective of influential west coast photographers including Ansel Adams and Edward Weston. The group mounted a 1932 exhibition at the de Young Museum in San Francisco, united by a manifesto declaring "photography as an art form by simple and direct presentation." Cunningham's vision came through in both her personal and commercial work: unvarnished celebrity portraits for *Vanity Fair*; documentary street photography; nudes and botanical images — a lifetime of work that continues to challenge and intrigue viewers.

Illustrated by Chandler O'Leary and printed by Jessica Spring, grateful for artists who remind us to focus. 164 copies were printed by hand at Springtide Press in Tacoma, March 2014

# Sadako Sasaki

Born January 7, 1943, in Japan; survived the atomic bombing of Hiroshima at age two ✦ Developed leukemia at age twelve as a result of radiation exposure ✦ Spent her days in the hospital folding origami cranes with a wish to live ✦ Died in 1955, buried with one thousand paper cranes

Sadako Sasaki was a maker—though she was motivated not by artistic drive but by a desperate hope. Sasaki is our youngest featured feminist; born in 1943, she lived just twelve years. Yet in that short time she made an impact on the world that will keep her legend alive forever.

At the age of two, Sasaki survived the atomic bombing of Hiroshima, Japan, that triggered the end of World War II. Though she was reportedly thrown through a window by the blast, she suffered no apparent injuries at the time. She did not come through the disaster unscathed, however. Shortly before her twelfth birthday, she began showing symptoms of what her mother called "an atom bomb disease." Soon afterward she was diagnosed with leukemia, and spent the remaining months of her life in a hospital room.

According to Japanese legend, a person who folds one thousand origami cranes will be granted a wish. Remembering this Sasaki began folding paper with single-minded determination, wishing simply to live. With her best friend Chizuko, she managed to finish 644 cranes before she lost her race with leukemia on October 25, 1955. In honor of her efforts, her classmates finished the remaining cranes and assembled them into a burial wreath for Sasaki. She is memorialized by the Children's Peace Monument, located in the center of Hiroshima—and like the origami cranes themselves, she is remembered today as a symbol of peace. The monument is inscribed with the words "This is our cry. This is our prayer. Peace in the world."

▲ These paper birds are strung together in what is called a *senbazuru*, which is traditionally given as a gift to newlyweds and newborns as a wish for a long life ahead.

◄ The *tanchozuru*, or red-crowned crane, is a symbol of luck and longevity in Japan. It is said to live for one thousand years, perhaps the origin of the origami crane legend.

▲ Sasaki is remembered with the Children's Peace Monument in Hiroshima. Hiroshi Oki, who contributed the Japanese calligraphy for our broadside, visited Hiroshima with his daughter Shiori, who shot these photographs.

S asaki relied on her imagination and creativity in the face of uncertainty and fear. The meditative act of folding hundreds of paper cranes must have felt comforting and productive to her, as otherwise she had no control over her illness. This act of creating something by hand while disaster looms is what inspired us to create our twelfth broadside, *Peace Unfolds*. When we received word that a magnitude 9.0 earthquake had hit Japan in March 2011, followed shortly afterward by a devastating tsunami and a meltdown at the Fukushima Daiichi Nuclear Power Plant, we felt a mounting dread and sense of powerlessness. Worst of all Japan was now reeling from a second nuclear disaster in just over sixty years.

We donated a portion of the proceeds from our broadside to Peace Winds, a Pacific Northwest organization with a dedicated relief and recovery fund for rebuilding Japan's infrastructure in affected areas. Yet what really inspired us was Sasaki's idea of imbuing paper with a wish—of creating something labor-intensive and meditative, and then sending it out into the world for a greater purpose—like a ripple becoming a tidal wave. Because of Sasaki's work, paper cranes have become forever linked to Hiroshima. So in honor of those lost and suffering in Japan following the Fukushima disaster—and with a wish for life, hope, and peace once again—we'd like to think of our edition of prints as a *senbazuru* of our own.

▲ One of the most famous pieces of Japanese art is the woodblock print *Great Wave Off Kanagawa* by Katsushiko Hokusai, which depicts a tsunami.

▲ The origami crane, or *orizuru*, is perhaps the best-known design of origami, the Japanese art of paper folding. It has become a symbol of peace, truth, longevity, and fidelity.

◄ Seattle's Peace Park centers around a life-size bronze statue of Sasaki. Dedicated on the forty-fifth anniversary of the Hiroshima bombing, Sasaki's statue is draped on the anniversary with thousands of paper cranes.

▲ *The Secret of One Thousand Cranes Paperfolding* (*Hiden Senbazuru Orikata*) is the first known book about origami, written in 1797.

**1** Our design honors *Cranes and New Year Sun*, a woodblock by Utagawa Hiroshige. His work referenced Hokusai's *Great Wave*.

**2** The other dominant color in our design is the plain white of the paper. The spare composition is an homage to Japanese aesthetic.

**3** Persimmon is often used to represent transformation and victory. The orange sun at the bottom of the print represents the modern Japanese flag.

**4** Our origami cranes fly upward and transform into real birds, symbolizing the transformation of Sasaki's wish into a tangible form of hope.

**5** *Peace Unfolds* is meant to be displayed vertically. To emphasize the Japanese calligraphy and the motion of the cranes, our text runs from bottom to top.

**6** Like the signature and "chop" on most Japanese prints, we included Sasaki's name and portrait. Her name is written in Japanese kanji by calligrapher Hiroshi Oki.

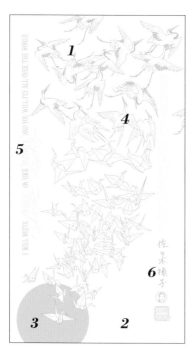

*"I will write peace on your wings and you will fly all over the world."*

## PEACE UNFOLDS

*No. 12 in the series*

**YEAR CREATED:** *2011*

**ISSUE:** *The 2011 earthquake and tsunami in Japan; the consequences of nuclear power and nuclear warfare*

**EDITION:** *166 prints; sixty-six years (at the time of printing) since the bombing of Hiroshima, Japan*

**DONATION:** *Peace Winds*

I WILL WRITE *peace* ON YOUR *WINGS*, AND YOU WILL FLY ALL OVER THE WORLD.

According to Japanese legend, one who folds 1000 origami cranes will be granted a wish. After being diagnosed with leukemia—a result of her proximity to the atomic bombing of Hiroshima—Sadako Sasaki (1943 – 1955) began folding paper, hoping to live. With her best friend Chizuko, she finished 644 cranes before her death at age 12. Sadako was buried with a wreath of 1000 cranes completed by her schoolmates, and is honored with the Children's Peace Monument in the center of Hiroshima.

Illustrated by Chandler O'Leary and printed by Jessica Spring, with kanji by Hiroshi Oki, in memory of those lost and suffering in Japan—and with a wish for hope, peace and life, once again. 166 copies were painted by hand at Springtide Press in Tacoma, May 2011

佐々木禎子

# Elizabeth Zimmermann

Born Elizabeth Lloyd-Jones in England on August 9, 1910; later called EZ by legions of knitting fans ✦ Immigrated to the United States with her husband, a German master brewer ✦ Revolutionized knitting instruction, encouraging knitters to develop their own patterns ✦ Popularized the use of circular needles ✦ Died in 1999; her "EPS" pattern formula is still used by knitting designers today

British-born master knitter Elizabeth Zimmermann (EZ) devoted her life to her craft and to teaching the joy of making to others. Since our series is imbued with hand-craftsmanship, we thought it only fitting to honor a woman whose hands were never idle.

Born in 1910 EZ first learned to knit from her mother and aunts, who taught her in the English style, where the yarn is held in the right hand and "thrown" over the needles for each stitch. Later her Swiss governess taught her the Continental technique, where the yarn is held in the left hand instead—making the entire process faster and more efficient. When she immigrated to the United States with her German husband, EZ found American knitters unaware of the Continental method and other knitting time-savers; this led her to begin teaching others to knit. She popularized the use of circular needles to create garments quickly and easily, and insisted that anyone could master the craft with the right tools and techniques.

To publish her knitting patterns and instruction books, EZ—along with her daughter Meg Swansen—founded Schoolhouse Press in a converted rural schoolhouse in Wisconsin. For the next four decades EZ inspired new generations of knitters with her innovative techniques and no-nonsense approach, through her books, magazine articles, in-person knitting retreats, and public television series.

EZ passed away in 1999, but Schoolhouse Press is still alive and well in the hands of Swansen. Thanks to the lifetime of patterns, books, and wisdom she left behind, modern knitters can find inspiration in EZ's motto: "Knit on with confidence and hope, through all crises."

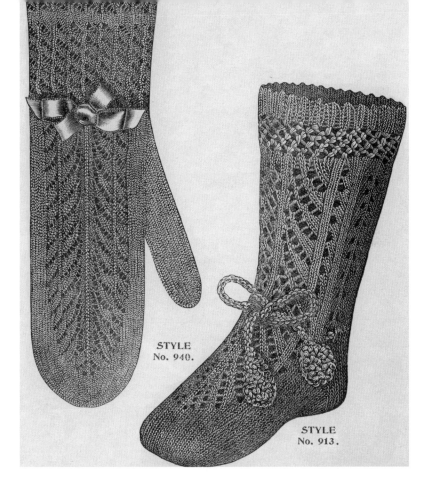

STYLE
No. 940.

STYLE
No. 913.

◄ Hand-knitting has been a
tradition for centuries. Many
modern knitters look to vintage
patterns for inspiration.

▲ EZ and her husband Arnold Zimmermann built
their marriage both as makers. Zimmermann was a
master brewer and EZ a textile craftswoman; each
was a successful entrepreneur.

◄ The EPS, or Elizabeth's Percentage System, is
a series of equations EZ developed for the design
of well-fitted garments. EPS ratios are designed to
make garment shaping nearly foolproof for a wide
variety of sizes and body types.

*I*f ever there was a discipline relegated to the category of "women's work," it is knitting. To this day knitting and other domestic crafts are often thought of as the domain of women—and rarely is knitting considered an art form. Yet EZ managed both to elevate her craft and bring it to the masses. She ran a successful business as a pattern drafter and knitting teacher, and her legacy has driven countless modern knitters to discover the beauty and value of creating handmade garments.

Our tenth Dead Feminists broadside, *Get Handy*, celebrates not just the art and craft of knitting, but the beauty of a handmade life. From master gardeners to woodworkers to home canners and slow-food chefs, the urban homesteading movement is rapidly gaining traction around the world, popularizing a return to hand-craftsmanship. The result is a thriving subculture of both women and men who resist the throwaway ethos of mass production and support a more sustainable way of life.

And the knitters of today? They are legion—and organized. Modern knitters are plugged into social media, sharing their designs and expertise with millions of like-minded makers. Many also use their craft and connections for the greater good, including the online group Knitters Without Borders, which raises funds for the healing hands of Nobel-laureate organization Médecins Sans Frontières (Doctors Without Borders). So in the spirit of lending a hand, we added a portion of our broadside proceeds to the cause. We think EZ would approve.

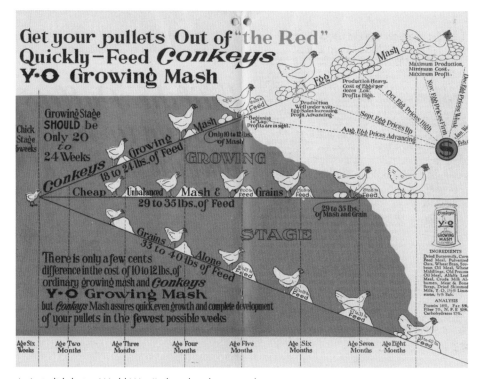

▲ As it did during World War II, the urban homesteading movement is gaining popularity. The movement includes hobbyists and professionals, embracing anyone dedicated to crafting a handmade life—one chicken coop at a time.

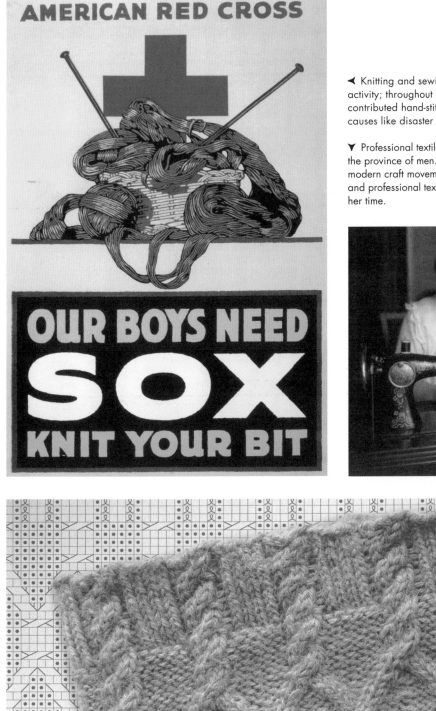

◄ Knitting and sewing is not just a domestic activity; throughout history, women have contributed hand-stitched goods to important causes like disaster relief and war efforts.

▼ Professional textiles have historically been the province of men. This is changing with the modern craft movement. EZ, both a home crafter and professional textile designer, was ahead of her time.

▲ Thanks to the trail blazed by EZ, many women have built their own businesses out of their love of knitting. These knitters design software and professional-quality patterns for other crafters.

**1** *Get Handy* celebrates the art of knitting—both the finished product and the process behind it.

**2** The piece is also a salute to the urban homesteading movement, which elevates domestic crafts to an art form.

**3** EZ was known for publishing simple geometric designs, but knitting also encompasses complex techniques, like Fair-Isle color patterning.

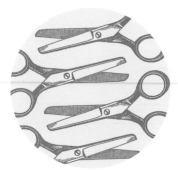

**4** Our design is full of hand-tools, from EZ's knitting needles to canning implements and woodworking materials. Every pair of hands needs the proper tools.

**5** To add even more of a handmade touch to the piece, the third color of sky blue was hand-painted.

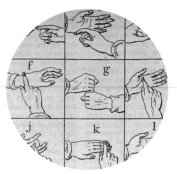

**6** Hidden in the design is a line of hands, spelling out the word "HANDY" in American Sign Language.

## "One tends to give one's fingers too little credit for their own good sense."

## GET HANDY

*No. 10 in the series*

**YEAR CREATED:** *2010*

**ISSUE:** *Urban homesteading and the value of hand-craftsmanship*

**EDITION:** *158 prints; EZ is credited with designing the first Aran or Fisherman's sweater for an American magazine, published in* Vogue Knitting *in 1958. Aran sweaters are distinguished by their use of complex textured stitch patterns.*

**DONATION:** *Medecins Sans Frontiéres (Doctors Without Borders) via Knitters Without Borders*

ELIZABETH ZIMMERMANN

ONE TENDS to GIVE one's fingers too little CREDIT FOR their own GOOD SENSE.

Elizabeth Lloyd-Jones Zimmermann (1910–1999) was a British-born master knitter. EZ (as she was known by legions of knitters) moved to the United States and founded Schoolhouse Press in the 1950s, teaching a new approach to knitting through original designs, newsletters, books and a television series. Her no-nonsense approach was laced with humor and readily applied to life beyond knitting, from encouragement in experimentation to trusting one's instincts. Americans were reintroduced to the easier, faster German or Continental style of knitting, which had fallen out of favor during WWII, while EZ encouraged students to think on their own using EPS (Elizabeth's Percentage System) to easily size garments. EZ's daughter Meg has continued her knitting legacy, most likely inspired by her mother's motto: "Knit on with confidence and hope, through all crises."

Illustrated by Chandler O'Leary and printed by Jessica Spring, continuously inspired by all the good deeds hands can do. 158 copies were printed by hand at Springtide Press in Tacoma. November 2010

Chandler O'Leary          22/158

VIRGINIA
··
WOOLF

RYWKA
··
LIPSZYC

SAROJINI
··
NAIDU

CHAPTER : 5

TELL

These women were all extraordinary storytellers. One woman meticulously composed her words, and then used them as building blocks on a page. Found in the ashes of Auschwitz, a young writer's diary survived to fulfill her dream of becoming a published writer. Another woman sang her stories to inspire and comfort a nation.

# VIRGINIA WOOLF

Born Adeline Virginia Stephen on January 25, 1882, in London ✦ Best known for her modernist novels including *Mrs. Dalloway, To the Lighthouse,* and *The Waves* ✦ Managed to recover her diaries after her London homes were damaged in the 1940 Blitz ✦ After a lifetime of struggling with mental illness, committed suicide by drowning in 1941

Books were an integral part of Virginia Woolf's life, and with unlimited access to her father's library, she decided to become a writer at an early age. In 1896 her mother died unexpectedly, triggering a mental breakdown for Woolf. Similar episodes would follow, shaping a life marked by the tragic loss of many family members and two world wars. All the same, life and work went on. Woolf married her husband, Leonard, in 1912. Around the same time a loose collective of friends and relatives established the informal Bloomsbury Group, named for the district in London where most of them lived. These writers, artists, and intellectuals rejected Victorian ideals, and instead supported gay rights, women's liberation, pacifism, uninhibited sexuality, and other—at the time—unconventional ideas.

In 1917 the Woolfs procured a handpress and established the Hogarth Press. Though self-taught Woolf had begun binding books at age nineteen. While Leonard printed, his hands too shaky for typesetting, Woolf became the type compositor: "You can't think how exciting, soothing, ennobling, and satisfying it is." They published their own writing, but also the work of T. S. Eliot, E. M. Forster, Fyodor Dostoyevsky, Katherine Mansfield, Vita Sackville-West, Sigmund Freud, as well as other members of the Bloomsbury Group. The work was often experimental and wouldn't have been published commercially without the Hogarth Press. Woolf had the opportunity to explore feminist themes absent in the literature written by men about women, as in the essay *A Room of One's Own*: "Some of the most inspired words and profound thoughts in literature fall from her lips; in real life she could hardly read; scarcely spell; and was the property of her husband." By 1924 the press had grown into a commercial venture, requiring employees and a move to larger quarters, but 34 of the 525 publications produced had been printed and bound by hand by the Woolfs.

▲ Woolf's 1919 short story "Kew Gardens" takes place in London's famous botanical garden, using the flower beds to anchor the story's themes of love, war, and the class system.

▲ In 1919 the Woolfs purchased Monk's House in Sussex for a country retreat. Shown here is Woolf's bedroom: "A woman must have money and a room of her own if she is to write fiction."

▶ Woolf had an affair in the 1920s with writer Vita Sackville-West, who identified herself—using the popular euphemism of the day—as a Sapphist. She inspired *Orlando*, Woolf's novel about a gender-crossing aristocrat.

Though the Hogarth Press was first established as a hobby, hopefully with therapeutic benefits for Woolf, the opportunity to be writer, editor, composer, and publisher was critical, completely informing her work. Free from editorial censorship and armed with the right tools, Woolf was playful with both form and composition. Tiny individual letters built words, words became blocks to compose, and the spaces between those blocks were considered with equal importance—this obviously informed her experimental approach as evidenced in her writing.

In 2011 we were invited to talk about the Dead Feminists series at the first Ladies of Letterpress conference. We revealed our thirteenth broadside at the event, a gathering of mostly women printers and bookmakers from around the country. Woolf, being an inspirational feminist *and* a letterpress printer, seemed like the perfect woman to bring with us. Meeting lots of eager young lady printers confirmed that a trade formerly dominated by men is now wide open to women, giving them a chance to run their own presses—and businesses—while fueling an incredible revival of the craft.

While we might not all have the chance to set type and run our own presses, we deserve the opportunity to tell our own stories free from censorship. While books aren't the only effective vehicle for sharing stories anymore, composing carefully crafted words remains the best way to make waves.

➤ Our donation went to the Independent Publishing Resource Center (IPRC) in Portland, Oregon, a non-profit organization that provides access to the resources and tools required for the creation of self-published media and art.

◄ In 1923 the Hogarth Press published T. S. Eliot's famous poem "The Waste Land," adding tremendously to their reputation. Woolf hand-set the entire poem, which she described as a typographic challenge.

▼ The Ladies of Letterpress conference gave us the chance to gather with women artists and printers—all in a room of our own.

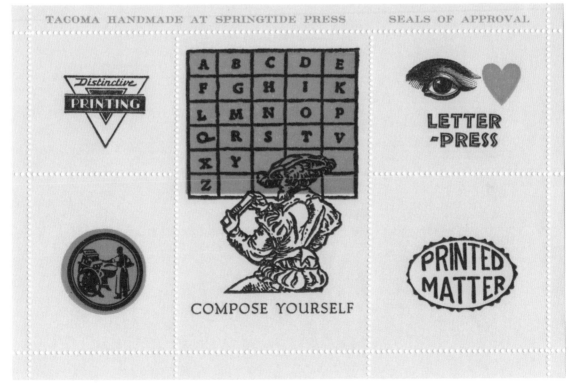

TACOMA HANDMADE AT SPRINGTIDE PRESS · · · SEALS OF APPROVAL

▲ Jessica's work often celebrates the craft of letterpress printing, as shown on these handset stamps that utilize cuts from the trade.

**1** The illustration references the Victorian era. The mirrors that spell out "Soul" reference a pattern by arts and crafts printer William Morris.

**2** Botanicals were a recurring theme in Woolf's work.

**3** We printed the broadside in ethereal metallic inks to give a subtle, ghostly glow to the piece and echo Woolf's sometimes melancholy life.

**4** Images of locked-up type inspired this Josephine Baker keepsake we created. Similarly composed type appears in *Paper Chase*.

**5** Using reference books like the popular *Language of Flowers*, people used to communicate their feelings by sending flowers in highly specific arrangements.

**6** The countries of the United Kingdom are represented by different plants: the rose of England, Northern Ireland's shamrock, the Scottish thistle, and the Welsh daffodil.

## *"Books are the mirrors of the soul."*

## PAPER CHASE

*No. 13 in the series*

**YEAR CREATED:** *2011*

**ISSUE:** *The continued relevance of physical books; women printers and authors; the importance of self-publishing*

**EDITION:** *129 prints; number of years (at the time of printing) since Woolf's birth*

**DONATION:** *Independent Publishing Resource Center*

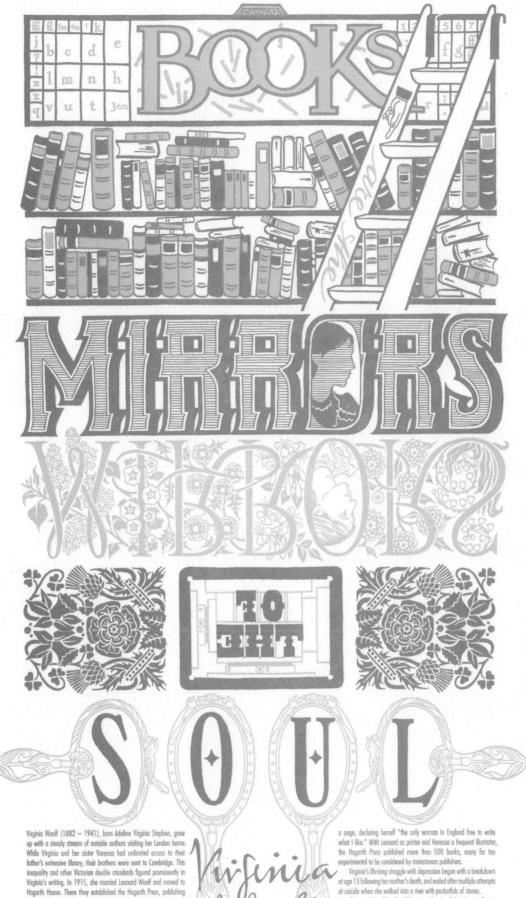

# BOOKS

# MIRRORS

# WINDOWS

# TO THE

# SOUL

Virginia Woolf (1882 – 1941), born Adeline Virginia Stephen, grew up with a steady stream of notable authors visiting her London home. While Virginia and her sister Vanessa had unlimited access to their father's extensive library, their brothers were sent to Cambridge. This inequality and other Victorian double standards figured prominently in Virginia's writing. In 1915, she married Leonard Woolf and moved to Hogarth House. There they established the Hogarth Press, publishing the work of T.S. Eliot, E.M. Forster, Vita Sackville-West, the first translations of Sigmund Freud as well as Virginia's own novels. As editor, typesetter and binder, Virginia had the freedom to control not just the content but the physicality of letterforms and space on a page, declaring herself "the only woman in England free to write what I like." With Leonard as printer and Vanessa a frequent illustrator, the Hogarth Press published more than 500 books, many far too experimental to be considered by mainstream publishers.

Virginia's life-long struggle with depression began with a breakdown at age 13 following her mother's death, and ended after multiple attempts at suicide when she walked into a river with pocketfuls of stones.

Illustrated by Chandler O'Leary and printed by Jessica Spring, with roots firmly planted in ink-and-paper soil, and souls bound to bloom. 129 copies were printed by hand at Springtide Press in Tacoma. August 2011

*Virginia Woolf*

Chandler O'Leary          28/129

# RYWKA LIPSZYC

Born September 15, 1929, in Poland; lived in Łódź Ghetto during World War II ✦ Lost both parents in the ghetto, left to look after three younger siblings ✦ Began a diary in 1943, while working as a factory seamstress ✦ Deported with her last-surviving sister and three cousins to Auschwitz in 1944; her cousins survived the war ✦ Believed to have died in 1945, shortly after Auschwitz was liberated, but no record of her fate survives

The story of Rywka Lipszyc* (pronounced "Rivka Lipschitz") is astonishing, if only for the fact that it can be told at all. Lipszyc was a teenager living in one of the worst Jewish ghettos of Nazi-occupied Poland during World War II. When she started her diary, she had already lost all but one of her immediate family members. She poured her heart and faith into the pages of her notebook, and documented everyday life in the ghetto. At times the diary is a harrowing account of hardship; at others it reads like the journal of any normal teenager. Just a few months after it begins, the diary ends abruptly—and with it most of our knowledge of Lipszyc's life. We know she was deported to Auschwitz, and that her sister was murdered upon arrival at the camp. Lipszyc was liberated by allied troops in 1945—but then her trail goes cold. The end of her story is a blank page.

What is truly remarkable is that the diary survived the war, the camps, and the intervening decades. A Russian army doctor allegedly found the diary in the ashes of the Auschwitz crematorium. She made a few margin notes, and then put it away in her closet at home—for the rest of her life. Upon her death her son found the diary, and then *he* stashed it away. When he died, his daughter traveled back to Russia from the United States and found the diary among his effects. She—the granddaughter of the army doctor—took it back to the United States, and turned it over to the Jewish Family and Children's Services Holocaust Center in San Francisco, where it was authenticated, translated, and published in 2014.

---

\* No surviving portraits of Lipszyc exist to our knowledge. This is an historical photo of a young seamstress in Łódź Ghetto.

▲ Prior to World War II, Łódź was home to over two hundred thousand Jews—one third of the city's total population. The Holocaust was responsible for all but wiping out the Jewish population there.

▼ Lipszyc's diary is a precious Holocaust artifact, but many ordinary traces of life in Łódź Ghetto also remain.

▲ Nazi-occupied Europe was dotted with ghettos—urban districts designed to confine and segregate Jewish citizens. Many, like those in Łódź and Warsaw, were enclosed with walls or fences, heavily guarded by soldiers.

One of the worst tragedies of the Holocaust was the silencing of the voices of millions of people. Few survived to tell the tale, and many of those who did could not bear to relive what happened. Accounts of what happened during the Holocaust, terrible as they are, are treasures—evidence of the truth, and proof that stories are our most important legacy.

Lipszyc is already being compared to Anne Frank, the other famous teenage diarist of the war. Yet Lipszyc provides a new point of view and previously unknown details of everyday life in Łódź Ghetto. Also, while Frank's diary is secular, Lipszyc's is quite religious. Her lyrical imagery and use of metaphor create an eloquent expression of her Jewish faith. Most poetic and haunting of all, the emergence of Lipszyc's journal secured her a place in the pantheon of writers.

We intended to release our Rywka Lipszyc broadside in time for the seventieth anniversary of the liberation of Auschwitz. Yet world events affected our plans in a profound way. In early January 2015 anti-Semitic terrorists in Paris attacked both a Jewish market and the offices of *Charlie Hebdo*, an incendiary satirical magazine. Twelve people were murdered, including five of the magazine's cartoonists. The incident appears to have been an attempt to stifle free speech; afterward, writers and artists around the world adopted the phrase *Je suis Charlie* in support of free expression. In that light we felt it was especially important to tell Lipszyc's tale, our own *Je suis Rywka*.

▲ In memory of those lost in the Paris attacks and to help fight anti-Semitism worldwide, we donated a portion of our proceeds to the Anti-Defamation League—a top human- and civil-rights organization for over one hundred years.

▲ A page from Lipszyc's diary.

▼ Lipszyc and Frank were not the only young diarists to document their Holocaust experiences. What began as simple children's narratives have become important historical records of the atrocities perpetrated by Nazi Germany.

▼ Memorials like this one in Boston, which lists victims only by their tattoo numbers, are poignant reminders of the countless personal stories lost or erased by the Holocaust.

*1* The border is reminiscent of embroidered textiles significant to Jewish culture.

*2* Ceremonial items like this marriage *ketubah* were taken away from Jewish families during the war.

*3* The floral motif recognizes Lipszyc's dual heritage, in a nod to traditional Polish folk art.

*4* The pink stitched lines represent Lipszyc's trade as a seamstress, which kept her alive and hopeful for worklife after the war.

*5* The delicate pale pastels and subtle metallic ink stand for the fragility and preciousness of life among the thorns of war and persecution.

*6* There is no surviving photograph of Lipszyc; the only visual she left behind was her handwriting.

*"Although life is difficult, it is also beautiful."*

## COMMON THREADS

*No. 21 in the series*

**YEAR CREATED:** *2015*

**ISSUE:** *Religious violence; seventieth anniversary of the Holocaust*

**EDITION:** *145 prints; Auschwitz was liberated in 1945*

**DONATION:** *Anti-Defamation League*

# ALTHOUGH LIFE IS DIFFICULT, IT IS ALSO *Beautiful*

## RYWKA LIPSZYC

Rywka Lipszyc (1929 – 1945?) kept a diary from
October 1943 to April 1944, while living in Poland's
Łódź ghetto. Discovered by a Russian doctor in the
crematoria remains at Auschwitz-Birkenau, the diary
was published in 2014, sharing Rywka's amazing story
with the world. Her parents and three siblings perished
in Nazi ghettos and killing centers. Despite horrible
living conditions Rywka survived, working in the ghetto's
clothing and linen workshop, learning to sew, organizing
a library, and attending classes. Her diary ends abruptly,
but records reveal she was deported to Auschwitz, then
liberated to a field hospital after the war's end. No further
trace of her has been found, but Rywka's words survive,
a reminder of her incredible faith despite all odds —
and her dream of becoming a writer fulfilled.

Illustrated by Chandler O'Leary and printed
by Jessica Spring, honoring words and images of
every faith as an invaluable thread that binds us
together. 145 copies were printed by hand at
Springtide Press in Tacoma. February 2015

CHANDLER O'LEARY    5/145

# SAROJINI NAIDU

Born Sarojini Chattopadhyay on February 13, 1879, in Hyderabad, India ✦ Came to be known as the Nightingale of India for her lyrical and nationalist poetry ✦ Was a key figure of the civil disobedience movement, and jailed along with Gandhi ✦ Led the Indian National Congress and became the first woman governor of Uttar Pradesh ✦ Died in 1949, two years after Indian independence; her birthday is celebrated as Women's Day in India

Like Rywka Lipszyc, Sarojini Naidu was defined by her words. Yet Naidu told her story—and the story of India—through verse. Though she famously said, "I am only a woman, only a poet," the Nightingale of India used words both to uplift and to lead her people.

From the time she was a young girl, Naidu was drawn to the power of words. She was a brilliant student, matriculating at Madras University at age twelve. At sixteen she traveled to England to study at King's College and Cambridge.

Her command of language made her a perfect match for writing; she was proficient in Urdu, Bengali, Telugu, English, and Persian. Focusing on Indian themes, she published several books of poetry, including *The Golden Threshold* (1905), *The Bird of Time* (1912), and *The Broken Wing* (1917). As her poems were originally published in English, they were popular with readers both in India and the United Kingdom.

Naidu's lyrical eloquence translated well to oration. When she returned from England, she became interested in politics and the Indian independence movement. Meeting Gandhi in 1916 inspired her to travel around India, speaking about women's emancipation and workers' rights. In 1925 she became the first Indian woman president of the Indian National Congress, and later joined the cause of civil disobedience with campaigns like the quit India movement, a mass protest demanding the end of British rule.

After hundreds of years of foreign rule, India finally gained its independence in 1947. For Naidu the victory was bittersweet—independence was merely the beginning of years of tension, conflict, and violence. Naidu died less than two years later, her political work unfinished. Yet her poetry leaves behind a comforting voice: "We will conquer the sorrow of life with the sorrow of song."

▲ Naidu dreamed of independence in her poem "To India": "Waken, O slumbering Mother and be crowned / Who once wert empress of the sovereign Past." Though her wish was fulfilled, peace was not to follow.

◄ Naidu's friendship with Mahatma Gandhi lasted decades. She campaigned with him on tour, supported him through his hunger strikes, and accepted the governorship of Uttar Pradesh with his encouragement.

**M**any of Naidu's poems speak eloquently of the power of dreams. Yet over and over again, the plans and dreams of so many women and girls are cut short by violence. In Naidu's home country of India, it is estimated that a crime against a woman is committed every three minutes—though Indian women are far from alone. Women all over the world fall prey to violence, and many crimes go unpunished—or even unreported.

Time and time again it has been proven that speaking out brings about change. Yet so much violence is aimed at silencing women, so empowering the victims of violence to report assaults and face their accusers is a constant uphill battle. In many countries women are seen as unreliable witnesses, and victims are accused of promiscuity and shamed or blamed for what they have endured. In addition it is difficult to convince the justice system to take these crimes seriously, and often criminal evidence is not collected properly. The only way to break the cycle is to encourage women to speak up, and pressure authorities to prosecute each and every reported crime.

We released our Sarojini Naidu broadside a few months after the terrible and widely publicized 2012 gang rape of a young Delhi woman on a private bus. She died of her injuries days later, and the public outcry was heard around the world. As a result of the high-profile case and the nationwide protests that followed, India has since made changes to investigation procedures for sexual assault cases, as well as stricter sentencing laws for perpetrators. Reporting of incidents by victims has increased since 2012, and the Indian media has committed to reporting every new rape case.

These changes are only the beginning, however. Naidu used her voice to speak out for her people, her words singing out loud and clear the way a nightingale fills the night air with song. We, too, must raise the cry for the victims of violence, to end the silence once and for all.

➤ This poster, created under the US Works Progress Administration, illustrates the power of artists to give voice to political issues.

◄ This seventeenth-century Indian painting depicts women performing a devotional offering. In honor of Naidu, we made our donation to Take Back the Night—a nonprofit seeking to end all forms of domestic and sexual crimes.

▼ Naidu's poetry lends a poignant perspective to the choices women make daily:

> "Give me to drink each joy and pain
> Which Thine eternal hand can mete,
> For my insatiate soul can drain
> Earth's utmost bitter, utmost sweet."

▲ At the age of nineteen, Naidu married Govindarajulu Naidu in an intercaste marriage. At the time such marriages were not allowed, but the couple enjoyed the blessing of their families and a long, happy life together.

# TAKE A CLOSER LOOK AT *NIGHTSONG*

*1* The illustrations are done in a graphic style similar to the figures and botanicals in Indian illuminated manuscripts.

*2* The illustration depicts a lush dream menagerie, with a variety of Indian birds and animals arrayed in mirror-image symmetry.

*3* The style of typography is reminiscent of Indian letterforms.

*4* Intricate patterns printed in rich brown ink were inspired by the ornate designs of Indian *mehndi* tattoos, traditionally painted with a long-lasting natural henna dye.

*5* We achieved the bright rainbow hues of the piece by using the split-fountain or "rainbow roll" process, where different colors of ink blend on the press.

*6* The nightingale's plaintive song is often associated with the power of poetry and human expression. Sappho called the "sweet-voiced" bird "spring's messenger."

## "What hope shall we gather, what dreams shall we sow?"

## NIGHTSONG

*No. 18 in the series*

**YEAR CREATED:** *2013*

**ISSUE:** *Violence against women*

**EDITION:** *147 prints; India gained its independence in 1947*

**DONATION:** *Take Back the Night*

WHAT · HOPE
Shall We Gather,
what
DREAMS
Shall we sow?

*Sarojini Naidu*

Sarojini Chattopadhyay Naiju (1879 – 1949),
also known as "The Nightingale of India," was born in Hyderabad,
the eldest of eight children. She was a gifted student, proficient in five languages, and by age 16
left the country to attend King's College to pursue her interest in poetry. Inspired by the suffragist
movement in England, she joined the struggle for Indian independence, traveling the country
to lecture on social welfare, women's rights and nationalism. Naidu played a leading role during
the Civil Disobedience Movement and was jailed along with Ghandi. Naidu wrote beautiful lyrical poetry,
focused on Indian themes, to inspire the nation. She was the first woman to serve as president of the Indian
National Congress, and the first woman to become the Governor of the state of Uttar Pradesh. Though Naidu humbly
claimed, "I am only a woman, only a poet," her birthday is celebrated as Women's Day throughout India.

Illustrated by Chandler O'Leary and printed by Jessica Spring, calling for an end to violence against women all over the world.
147 copies were printed by hand at Springtide Press in Tacoma. August 2013

CHANDLER O'LEARY                    5/147

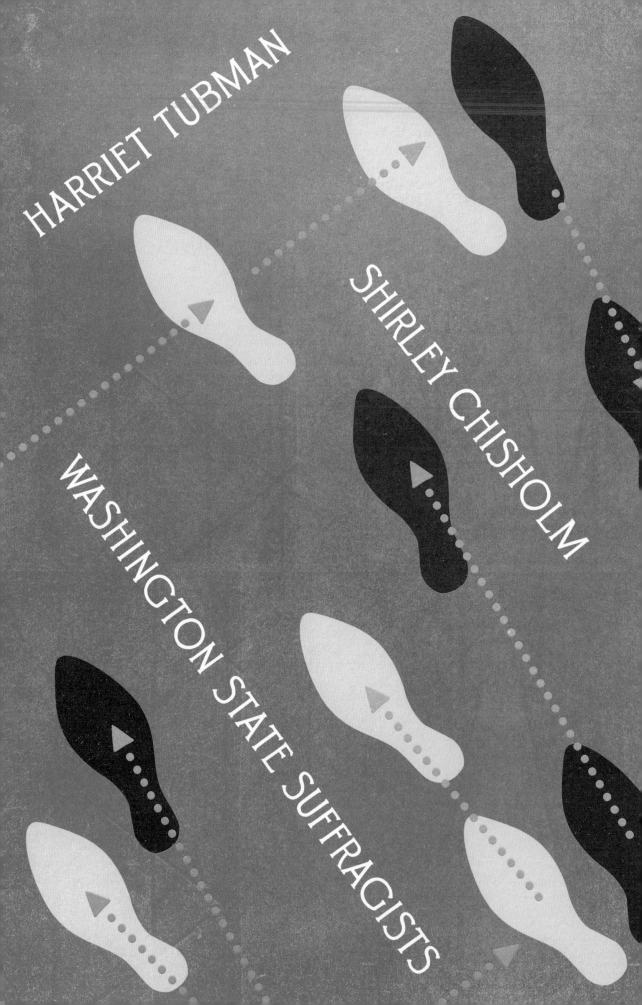

HARRIET TUBMAN

SHIRLEY CHISHOLM

WASHINGTON STATE SUFFRAGISTS

# CHAPTER 6

# LEAD

All of our dead feminists are leaders, but these women especially forged the way for the rest of us to follow. One woman escaped slavery, and then conducted other slaves to freedom. Sixty years later Washington suffragists reached across party lines to win women their right to vote, and in another sixty years a woman ran for president of the United States.

# HARRIET TUBMAN

Born Araminta Ross circa 1822 in Maryland; took her mother's name, Harriet ✦ Nicknamed "Moses"; guided freedom seekers on the Underground Railroad ✦ Served as a nurse, cook, spy, recruiter, and raid leader for the Union Army ✦ Worked for women's suffrage with Susan B. Anthony ✦ Died in 1913 at the Harriet Tubman Home for the Aged, which she founded

Born a slave Harriet Tubman spent her childhood working in the fields. When she was twelve years old, she suffered a blow to the head while trying to protect a slave boy from their overseer, and though she survived, she had ongoing headaches and seizures. Tubman's injury caused visions, inspiring both strong faith and perhaps the motivation to flee to freedom.

In 1849 she escaped north traveling via the Underground Railroad to Philadelphia. Once free Tubman returned to Maryland to lead others to freedom, including most of her family. Despite her small stature, she was a strong leader, armed with a hymnal of favorite spirituals and a small pistol to provide both protection and motivation for those slaves too weary and fearful to continue their journey north. In addition to her skills as a leader, Tubman relied on her cleverness and experience—varying her routes, traveling at night, wearing disguises, and following the river and stars to head north.

Tubman's experience acquired as a conductor on the Underground Railroad and her commitment to end slavery made her a perfect spy for the Union Army. She recruited slaves to fight, and in 1863 she became the first woman to command a military raid, guiding Colonel Montgomery and his regiment up the Combahee River to destroy Confederate supply lines and liberate more than seven hundred slaves.

Following the war Tubman worked fervently as a humanitarian and activist back in New York. She raised funds for the Freedman's Bureau to support and educate newly freed slaves, and built a retirement home on her property in Auburn. Tubman was a frequent speaker at local and national suffrage conventions, collaborating with movement leaders and abolitionists—including Susan B. Anthony, Elizabeth Cady Stanton, and Lucretia Mott.

◀ Launching of the *SS Harriet Tubman* in June 1944, the first Liberty ship named for a Black woman.

▼ Routes of the Underground Railroad, 1830–1865, show a network of secret routes and safe houses used by slaves for escape to free states and Canada.

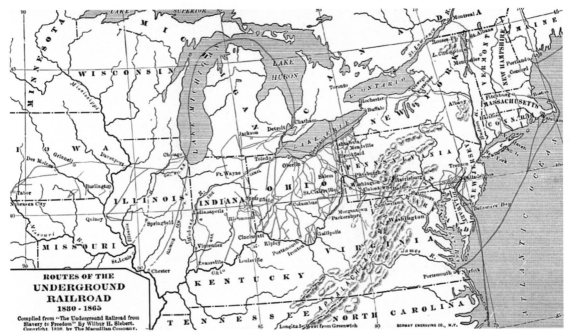

ROUTES OF THE
UNDERGROUND
RAILROAD
1830 - 1865

Compiled from "The Underground Railroad from
Slavery to Freedom" By Wilbur H. Siebert.
Copyright 1898, by The Macmillan Company.

**T**ubman is a legend, and the details of her story are well-known, taught to children in grade school. But like other heroines—including Sojourner Truth and Rosa Parks—the stories can eclipse the facts. These strong women leaders are so inspiring that various causes (including feminists) co-opt their stories, creating a larger-than-life mythology. Even the quote we featured in our broadside, long accepted as Tubman's words, has come into question in the years since we created our piece.

Recently published Tubman biographies question details from her 1868 biography—still the go-to source for much of her life story—which reported Tubman rescued three hundred people and made nineteen trips back to the South. W. E. B. DuBois claimed she rescued thousands of slaves and had a ten-thousand-dollar bounty for capture. While the true figures may be closer to seventy people in thirteen trips, this takes nothing away from Tubman's heroic status, especially understanding most slaves that *did* escape were young men, traveling alone. What we do know is based on Tubman's own words: "I was conductor of the Underground Railroad for eight years, and I can say what most conductors can't say—I never ran my train off the track and I never lost a passenger."

Stories about Tubman's heroism also fail to profile the last years of her life, when she was living nearly destitute, fighting to get her rightful soldier's pension. While the men she led during the Civil War were paid for their work, Tubman never was. Her attempts to recover back pay were fruitless, though in the 1890s she was finally awarded a nurse's pension. As we rely on amazing women like Tubman to inspire us to lead our own journeys, we must repay them as best we can by delving deeper and sharing their whole story.

▲ Women on 20s led a successful effort to put a woman on US currency, collecting half a million votes in 2014. The winner was Harriet Tubman, as imagined here. The last woman featured on US paper currency was Martha Washington in 1886.

SCENES

IN THE LIFE OF

HARRIET TUBMAN.

BY

SARAH H. BRADFORD.

AUBURN:
W. J. MOSES, PRINTER.

1869.

HARRIET TUBMAN.

▲ Sarah Hopkins Bradford wrote *Scenes in the Life of Harriet Tubman* in 1869 and *Harriet, the Moses of Her People* in 1886, both of which provided some financial support for Tubman.

▼ An advertisement offering bounties for "Minty" (Tubman's nickname) and her brothers Ben and Harry. Claims of a forty-thousand-dollar bounty, a figure which would be worth several million today, for Tubman were exaggerated.

**THREE HUNDRED DOLLARS REWARD.**

RANAWAY from the subscriber on Monday the 17th ult., three negroes, named as follows: HARRY, aged about 19 years, has on one side of his neck a wen, just under the ear, he is of a dark chestnut color, about 5 feet 8 or 9 inches hight; BEN, aged about 25 years, is very quick to speak when spoken to, he is of a chestnut color, about six feet high; MINTY, aged about 27 years, is of a chestnut color, fine looking, and about 5 feet high. One hundred dollars reward will be given for each of the above named negroes, if taken out of the State, and $50 each if taken in the State. They must be lodged in Baltimore, Easton or Cambridge Jail, in Maryland.

ELIZA ANN BRODESS,
Near Bucktown, Dorchester county, Md.
Oct. 3d, 1849.

☞ The Delaware Gazette will please copy the above three weeks, and charge this office.

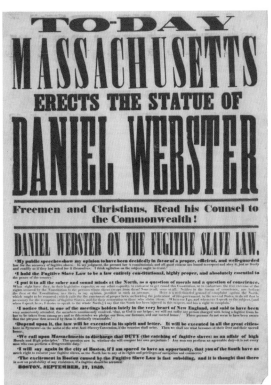

▲ The Underground Railroad spread with the passage of the Fugitive Slave Act in 1850, and escaped slaves continued north all the way to Canada to avoid recapture.

*1* The style of lettering is reminiscent of mid-nineteenth-century handbills and newspaper headlines.

*2* This was the first time we hand-colored one of our broadsides. The yellow details were hand-painted with watercolor.

*3* Typography can be oriented many ways on a page. To symbolize the difficulty of Tubman's treks, this broadside challenges the reader.

*4* Tubman sang songs at different tempos as signals to Underground Railroad passengers.

*5* Though current research has found no evidence, legend tells of coded quilts hung in windows that provided messages for passengers on the Underground Railroad.

*6* Before modern navigation aids arrived, constellations like the drinking gourd (a.k.a. the Big Dipper) guided travelers.

## *"Always remember you have within you the strength, the patience and the passion to reach for the stars to change the world."*

### END OF THE LINE

*No. 5 in the series*

**YEAR CREATED:** *2009*

**ISSUE:** *Bipartisanship and political cooperation*

**EDITION:** *146 prints; number of years (at the time of printing) since the Emancipation Proclamation*

**DONATION:** *No donations made this early in the series*

*Reach* **FOR** ★ **THE** ★ **STARS** ★ **TO CHANGE** ★ **WORLD** ★

**To**

**the STRENGTH the PATIENCE and the PASSION**

**HAVE WITHIN YOU**

**ALWAYS REMEMBER YOU**

**HARRIET TUBMAN**

Harriet Tubman (1820 – 1913) was born Araminta Ross as a slave in Maryland. In 1849 she escaped north traveling via the Underground Railway to Philadelphia. Once free, "Moses" made 19 more round trips — guiding nearly 300 slaves to freedom — and she "never lost a passenger." During the Civil War, Tubman recruited slaves to fight for the Union Army and led the Combahee River expedition to free more than 750 people. After the war she continued to work tirelessly for the rights of women and African Americans.

Illustrated by Chandler O'Leary and printed by Jessica Spring, who believe that cooperation and hope give us the momentum to reach the end of the line — without losing any passengers. 146 copies were printed by hand at Springtide Press, way up north in Tacoma. August 2009.

CHANDLER O'LEARY          78/146

# WASHINGTON STATE SUFFRAGISTS

Washington State voters approved a constitutional amendment on November 8, 1910, legalizing women's suffrage ✦ Susan B. Anthony helped form the Washington Equal Suffrage Association (WESA) in the 1870s ✦ Officers included: Emma Smith DeVoe (1848–1927) from Tacoma, May Arkwright Hutton (1860–1915) from Spokane, Dr. Cora Smith Eaton (1867–1939) from Seattle, and Bernice A. Sapp (1881–1965) from Olympia

Our home state of Washington was the fifth in the nation to give women the vote, and the movement succeeded as a result of many leaders working together despite much head butting, personality clashing, and partisan infighting. While women had the right to vote when Washington was still a territory, statehood and clashes with temperance supporters disenfranchised women all over again in 1888. The first president of WESA, Emma Smith DeVoe, came to Tacoma in 1905 to reinvigorate the state's campaign, having worked for the National American Woman Suffrage Association. She brought plenty of political experience and tactics ranging from parades to posters and publicity stunts, all delivered with a polite "ladylike" approach. Treasurer Cora Smith Eaton was a practicing doctor and founding member of The Mountaineers, eventually climbing six of the state's largest mountains. Auditor Bernice Sapp meticulously recorded and indexed all the group's letters and manuscripts, creating an invaluable archive.

From the east side of the state came Vice President May Arkwright Hutton, a self-made woman who strongly supported workingwomen and labor. In contrast to DeVoe, Hutton preferred a one-on-one approach, foregoing public demonstrations, though her outspoken demeanor was viewed by the other women as too coarse, citing her "former life and reputation" in an attempt to force her out of WESA.

Despite their differences, the WESA officers worked together to produce the *Washington Women's Cook Book*, published in 1908, and reprinted in 1909 for the Alaska-Yukon-Pacific (AYP) Exposition. Serving as both a fundraising tool and propaganda for the movement, the small but mighty cookbook includes everything from sailor's and vegetarian recipes to instructions for building a campfire. A true collaboration, it included recipes from women around the country with inspiring quotes for suffragists and potential supporters of their cause. While the intended audience was women, the authors cleverly recognized that the way to a man's heart—or vote—is through his stomach.

▲ Sapp, former chief researcher for the State Capital Museum in Olympia, working as a state supreme court clerk in 1914.

▲ Hutton moved to Spokane in 1906 determined to win suffrage for women, having already been a voter since 1896 in Idaho.

◄ In July 1909 suffrage proponents from across the country gathered in Seattle to celebrate Woman Suffrage Day at Washington's first world's fair, the AYP Exposition at the University of Washington.

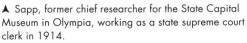

The Dead Feminists series began before Obama's election, and his victory ended eight years of conservative control. We had high hopes for the passage of progressive causes, but filibustering and partisanship essentially shut the government down. It was around this time when we started researching a suffrage leader to portray in our next print. When we discovered the *Washington Women's Cook Book*, it was clear we were on the right track, as evidenced in the dedication page: "To the first woman who realized that half of the human race were not getting a square deal, and who had the courage to voice a protest; and also to the long line of women from that day unto this, who saw clearly, thought strongly, and braved misrepresentation, ridicule, calumny, and social ostracism, to bring about that millennial day when humanity shall know the blessedness of dwelling together as equals."

The opportunity to research the archives at the Washington State Library in Olympia was incredibly helpful, and the experience inspired us to begin donating to applicable causes. Despite being in the midst of severe funding cutbacks and pending layoffs, the librarians took the time to help us explore DeVoe's archives. *Just Desserts* was inspired by the one hundredth anniversary of Washington suffrage, and our admiration for women who could cooperate despite differences in social class, education, and even demeanor, as they literally stirred the pot.

➤ In 2010 the state capitol hosted a centennial celebration of women's suffrage, including costumed interpreters, reenactments of house debates, and a "Votes for Women" photo booth.

▲ The 1920 election became the first US presidential election in which women were permitted to vote in every state.

▼ We spent hours sifting through the archives, and came to know each member by her quirks. Eaton took notes on her prescription pad and Sapp saved even the most mundane correspondence.

▲ On the one hundredth anniversary of women's suffrage in Washington State, we created a large linoleum carving honoring Eaton's climb to place the "Votes for Women" flag at the summit of Mt. Rainier.

*1* Molded gelatin desserts were a Victorian favorite. The "J" from the original Jell-O box design makes a cameo in the print.

*2* Our layering of translucent pink, blue, and yellow ink allowed us to create a full rainbow.

*3* *Just Desserts* hearkens back to the days of leaflet campaigning.

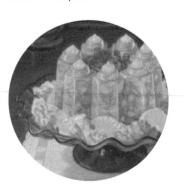

*4* We were amused by the penchant of vintage recipes to suspend a variety of objects in gelatin.

*5* Along the border is a real recipe (though we don't recommend you try it at home), handwritten like the faded recipe cards of our mothers and grandmothers.

*6* Molded desserts enjoyed a resurgence in the mid-twentieth century—which gave us plenty of food for thought and lots of kitschy inspiration.

> *"Are not our desserts and salads things of beauty and the joy of the moment?"*

## JUST DESSERTS

*No. 7 in the series*

**YEAR CREATED:** *2010*

**ISSUE:** *Bipartisanship and political compromise*

**EDITION:** *One hundred prints; the centennial of women's suffrage in Washington State*

**DONATION:** *Washington State Library, which houses the entire collection of papers and correspondence of the state's suffragist movement and the four women we researched (we began our tradition of making donations with* Just Desserts*)*

ARE NOT OUR

DESSERTS

SALADS things OF beauty AND·THE JOY OF THE MOMENT?

season high with pepper and salt, strain, add gelatine (dissolved) and fill mould. When cold cut in slices or cubes and serve with lettuce leaves with mayonnaise.

One can tomatoes, one-half box gelatine, pepper and salt. Boil tomatoes,

Tomato Jelly Salad.

In 1909 suffragists saw an opportunity to forward their cause in Seattle at the Alaska-Yukon-Pacific (AYP) Exposition. The Washington Equal Suffrage Association (WESA), led by president Emma Smith DeVoe, provided an AYP exhibition on the importance of women's right to vote and hosted Women's Days, distributing pamphlets alongside displays of domesticity. WESA treasurer Dr. Cora Smith Eaton joined The Mountaineers' AYP expedition to climb Mt. Rainier and placed a "Votes for Women" banner at the summit. Suffragists from eastern Washington, led by May Arkwright Hutton, came by the trainload to attend the AYP and WESA's National Convention. Many of the details — from ideological clashes to victories — were archived at the Washington State Library, thanks to Bernice Sapp.

Women from around the country also contributed to the *Washington Women's Cook Book*, published to sell at the AYP. Filled with recipes, domestic advice and inspirational suffragist quotes, it reassured male voters that the women in their lives would continue homemaking once they had the right to vote: "Give us the vote and we will cook, the better for a wide outlook." Compiled by Linda Deziah Jennings, the preface extolled the virtues of making beautiful things, and the simple joy of desserts and salads. Suffragists in Washington worked through differences in personalities, social backgrounds and political parties to create a winning recipe, gaining their right to vote in 1910.

Illustrated by Chandler O'Leary and printed by Jessica Spring with gratitude to *all* the cooks. 100 copies were printed by hand at Springtide Press in Tacoma. February 2010

May Arkwright Hutton ❦ Bernice Sapp ❦ Cora Smith Eaton ❦ Emma Smith DeVoe

CHANDLER O'LEARY    1/100

# SHIRLEY CHISHOLM

Born Shirley Anita St. Hill on November 30, 1924 ✦ Denied admittance to a club at Brooklyn College; she founded Ipothia (In Pursuit of the Highest in All) ✦ Following the failure to pass the ERA, helped found the National Women's Political Caucus in 1971 ✦ Her quote "I breathe fire" earned her the nickname "Pepperpot" ✦ Died in 2005; when asked how she'd like to be remembered, said, "I'd like them to say Shirley Chisholm had guts"

Born the daughter of immigrants, Shirley Anita St. Hill Chisholm was born in the Bedford-Stuyvesant neighborhood of Brooklyn in New York City. She and her sisters spent their early years with their grandmother in Barbados on her farm. Chisholm credits her grandmother as a major influence, along with Eleanor Roosevelt. Roosevelt left the fourteen-year-old Chisholm invaluable advice that she definitely took to heart: "Don't let anybody stand in your way." Her interest in politics blossomed as a student at Brooklyn College, where she joined the Harriet Tubman Society, debated, and attended community meetings.

After earning a master's degree at Columbia University, she became an educational consultant in New York City's Bureau of Child Welfare from 1959 to 1964 while still actively engaged in community and civic activities including the NAACP, the League of Women Voters, and the Bedford-Stuyvesant Political League, an organization formed to support Black candidates. Chisholm's confrontational style made her unpopular with the white Democratic establishment in New York, but her community—predominantly Black and Hispanic—gave her all the support she needed to win a seat in the state assembly in 1964. The people chose Chisholm, and she worked hard for them, focusing on education issues from day care to college, as well as gaining job security for teachers on maternity leave.

In 1968 Chisholm ran for Congress, becoming the first Black woman to serve in the House. Assigned to the Forestry Committee, she demanded reassignment to better represent her constituency. Moved to Veterans' Affairs, she staunchly refused to take money away from children and the disadvantaged for defense spending. In 1972 Chisholm ran for US president, the first woman and Black candidate on a major party ticket. Though she didn't win a single primary, she was truly "a catalyst for change," leading 152 delegates to the Democratic Convention.

➤ At the Democratic Convention Chisholm delivered her delegates to George McGovern—who lost to Richard Nixon in a landslide.

**supersisters**™ 71

**SHIRLEY CHISHOLM**

▲ Chisholm's antiestablishment congressional campaign, "Unbought and Unbossed," succeeded with major support from women and Puerto Rican voters, the latter whom she often addressed in Spanish.

▼ A founding member of the Congressional Black Caucus in 1971 and the Women's Caucus six years later, Chisholm served seven terms in Congress.

C hisholm was one of fifteen presidential candidates in 1972. It was a volatile time: the Vietnam War was the center of public discord, movements for civil rights and gender equality were major issues around the Western world, and the election came on the heels of the 1968 race— one of the bloodiest election years in American history. Chisholm knew she was a long shot; she even referred to herself as "literally and figuratively the dark horse." But she knew that if she played it smart and started winning delegates, she'd have some power to leverage.

Chisholm sought to create a truly representative government. She also saw her office as an opportunity to encourage women—especially women of color—to get involved in politics. Every member of her staff was a woman, half of them Black. On the national political stage, however, her race and gender were two strikes against her. She gathered support from the National Organization for Women, but when the time came for NOW to officially endorse a candidate, their squeamishness over the possibility of a Black nominee overcame their lip service. And the Black Congressional Caucus, of which Chisholm was a founding member, couldn't bring themselves to support a female candidate. Chisholm said in her "Equal Rights for Women" speech, "As a Black person, I am no stranger to race prejudice. But the truth is that in the political world I have been far oftener discriminated against because I am a woman than because I am Black." Her refusal to accept the status quo and run for office against all odds shows incredible leadership, decades before Barack Obama's two-term presidency. Chisholm wrote in 1973: "The next time a woman runs, or a Black, or a Jew, or anyone from a group that the country is 'not ready' to elect to its highest office, I believe that he or she will be taken seriously from the start . . . I ran because somebody had to do it first."

In honor of Chisholm's long-term service to her home city, we donated to Bedford-Stuyvesant Restoration, the nation's first nonprofit community development corporation. Restoration partners with residents and businesses to improve the quality of life of central Brooklyn by fostering economic self-sufficiency, enhancing family stability, promoting the arts and culture, and transforming the neighborhood into a safe, vibrant place to live and work.

◄ In 2004 director Shola Lynch produced *Chisholm '72: Unbought and Unbossed*, documenting Chisholm's campaign.

▼ Chisholm looks on as President Gerald Ford signed legislation declaring Women's Equality Day on August 26, 1974. Other onlookers include Barbara Jordan, Bella Abzug, and Betty Ford.

◄ When her opponent George Wallace was wounded in an assassination attempt, Chisholm visited him in the hospital. Years later Wallace used his clout among Southern congressmen to help Chishom pass a minimum-wage bill.

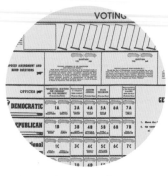

**1** As a nod to voting obstructions like literacy tests and hanging chads, our ballot spells out part of the quote in a Scantron.

**2** The US map hidden in the illustration is a reimagined reference to the 1972 Electoral College map—which then was a sea of red.

**3** In honor of Chisholm's smart style and sense of humor, we used playful typefaces and lettering styles to get her serious message across.

**4** There are way too many women who fought their whole lives for our right to vote; Chisholm's quote was the perfect reminder before the 2012 election.

**5** The color scheme is a retro seventies twist on the classic presidential red, white, and blue.

**6** Our very first Dead Feminists broadside threw our support behind President Obama and his campaign mantra of "Change." *Keep the Change* references that slogan.

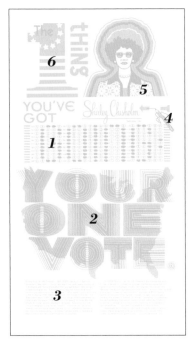

## "The one thing you've got going: your one vote."

### KEEP THE CHANGE

*No. 16 in the series*

**YEAR CREATED:** *2012*

**ISSUE:** *2012 presidential election and the power of voting*

**EDITION:** *152 prints; the number of delegates Chisholm won during the 1972 presidential primaries*

**DONATION:** *Bedford-Stuyvesant Restoration, Chisholm's home district, to continue support after Hurricane Sandy*

# The 1 thing

## YOU'VE GOT

*Shirley Chisholm*
Write In

## YOUR ONE VOTE

Shirley Anita St. Hill Chisholm (1924–2005) was born in Bedford-Stuyvesant, New York — though she spent her early years growing up in Barbados with her grandmother and younger sisters. She earned a master's degree from Columbia University and moved on to teach, becoming an authority on early education. After working as a consultant to the Bureau of Child Welfare, Chisholm won a seat in the New York State Assembly in 1964. She ran for the House of Representatives in 1968 under the slogan "Unbought and Unbossed," and was the first African-American woman elected to Congress. As a junior member, she was assigned to the House Forestry Committee but demanded reassignment on the grounds that she couldn't effectively represent her inner-city constituency. A founding member of the Congressional Black Caucus, she served seven terms in Congress.

In 1972 Chisholm ran for U.S. President, the first woman and African American on a major party ticket. She fiercely supported the rights of women and people of color; and opposed the Vietnam War. She was "literally and figuratively the dark horse"— women voters limited their support based on race, and the Congressional Black Caucus backed off because of her gender. Though she didn't win a single primary, she proved "a catalyst for change," gathering 152 delegates and demonstrating that women could compete nationally. Chisholm ended her campaign at the Convention, releasing her delegates to George McGovern — who lost in a landslide to Richard Nixon.

Illustrated by Chandler O'Leary and printed by Jessica Spring. Please vote to keep women moving forward. 152 copies were printed by hand at Springtide Press in Tacoma. November 2012

CHANDLER O'LEARY                    33/152

BABE ZAHARIAS

MARIE CURIE

SAPPHO

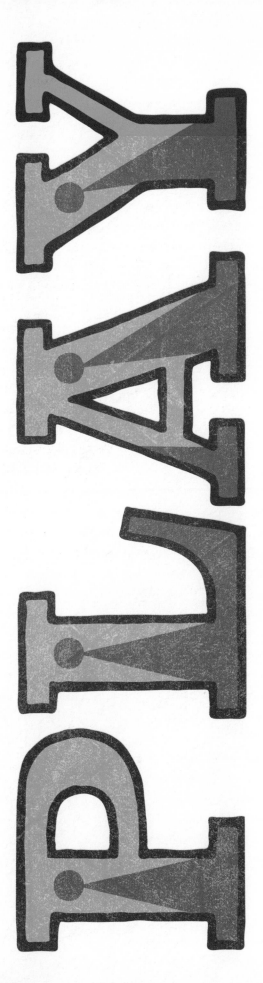

# CHAPTER 7

The word *play* meant something different to each of the women in this chapter. One was a player in the traditional sense, a master athlete for whom play was serious business. For another play meant experimentation, a trial-and-error approach to science. For the third wordplay was her trade and her legacy.

# BABE ZAHARIAS

Born Mildred Ella Didrikson on June 26, 1911, in Port Arthur, Texas ✦ Earned her nickname as a child playing baseball with neighborhood boys, supposedly inspired by slugger Babe Ruth ✦ Was a champion at many different sports, not just one ✦ Best known as a golfer; won an unprecedented seventeen straight women's amateur victories ✦ Died of cancer in 1953 at the age of forty-five

Babe Didrikson Zaharias was the consummate player, an athlete and entertainer still unrivaled to this day. A born athlete, she tried her hand at a wide range of sports and mastered them all. Today it's remarkable for an athlete to be proficient at two sports, but Zaharias excelled at nearly a dozen, including basketball, track and field, tennis, diving, bowling, billiards, and archery. Her prowess was matched only by her bravado. When entering a competition, she often declared: "The Babe is here. Who's coming in second?"

In 1932 she entered an amateur track-and-field championship as a one-woman squad, finishing first in five events and tying for first in a sixth. She single-handedly racked up thirty team points. The second-place team scored only twenty-two points—with twenty-two team members competing. The event qualified her for the Olympics the same year, where she competed and medaled in three track events. Her medal count was so low only because, at the time, an athlete could enter a maximum of three events.

Zaharias was best known as a golfer and founding member of the LPGA. Despite coming to the sport relatively late in her career, she blew away the competition with a winning streak that remains unsurpassed. Even after she was diagnosed with rectal cancer and underwent a colostomy, she won the US Women's Open just a year after her surgery. Her life was cut short by her illness, but she is still unmatched on the playing field. In 1999 the Associated Press named her Woman Athlete of the Twentieth Century, but Zaharias was a champion who transcended gender.

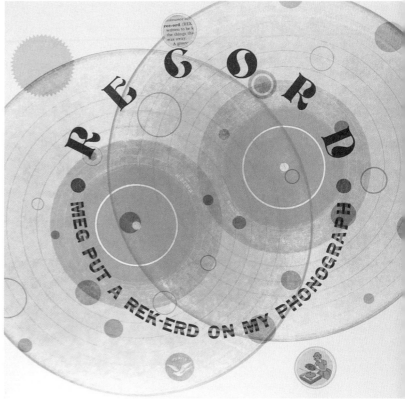

▲ Zaharias was a latecomer to golf, but it quickly became her best and favorite sport. She once said, "I expect to play golf until I am ninety—even longer if anybody figures out a way to swing a club from a rocking chair."

➤ Zaharias was famous during her lifetime, but few people know she was also a performer and singer. She once toured with a Vaudeville troupe, and even recorded songs on the Mercury Records label.

n Zaharias's lifetime she was hampered by a host of restrictions on women competitors, and plagued by a media that ignored her accomplishments. Instead the press focused on her tomboyish looks, brash demeanor, and (lack of) relationship status. The pressure was relentless: the *New York World-Telegram* wrote, "It would be much better if she and her ilk stayed at home, got themselves prettied up, and waited for the phone to ring."

Even Zaharias, known for her arrogant showboating and fiercely competitive nature, started wearing lipstick and more feminine clothing. Many have even argued that she switched to golf and married George Zaharias simply to conform to societal expectations to look and act more ladylike. She certainly treated these changes as a media makeover—perhaps to get the press off her back and shift the focus back to her abilities.

We couldn't help but wonder how Zaharias's career might have been different if "pretty" weren't a factor—if she could have been recognized and remembered for who she was, rather than what she wasn't. Unfortunately, women athletes still face this sort of battle today. All of this makes legislation like Title IX—intended to end gender discrimination in American education—incredibly important, even all these years later. Women athletes make a fraction of the salaries of their male counterparts; to this day many sports have no official female equivalent. So to help give girls everywhere equal access to sports and athletic training, we supported the Women's Sports Foundation with our broadside proceeds. Founded in 1974 by tennis legend Billie Jean King, the Women's Sports Foundation works to advance the lives of girls and women through physical activity.

➤ Zaharias's greatest friend and companion was Betty Dodd, her fellow golfer and protégé. After Zaharias's cancer diagnosis, Betty moved in with her and George for the last years of her life. Their relationship, while certainly intimate, was never publicly acknowledged.

# FIELD DAY

W.P.A. RECREATION
PROJECT DISTRICT No. 2

Gossard
*Corsets and Brassieres*

*The Gossard Line of Beauty*

The H. W. Gossard Co., Chicago, New York, San Francisco, Toronto, London, Sydney, Buenos Aires

▲ The controversy and speculation over Zaharias's personal life often overshadowed her accomplishments on the playing field. Mentioned only in lists of great women players, she outranks many male athletes.

◄ Zaharias was a square peg all her life, never quite fitting into the gender roles and expectations of her time. For all her brashness, she was self-conscious about her image. "I know I'm not pretty," she once said, "but I try to be graceful."

# TAKE A CLOSER LOOK AT *TITLE NINE IRON*

*1* Our broadside design is gender-neutral, focusing instead on golf ephemera and icons.

*2* We created the piece while our hometown hosted the US Men's Open golf championship.

*3* While Zaharias was famous as a golfer, we didn't want to forget her origins as a track star.

*4* Zaharias's name is adorned with a nine-iron club, symbolic of the Title IX legislation.

*5* We chose a color scheme that represents both the traditional trappings of golf and Zaharias's bold personality.

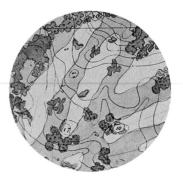

*6* In homage to the iconic anatomy of the golf course, our illustration is decked out in fairways and putting greens.

## "It's not enough just to swing at the ball. You've got to loosen your girdle and let 'er fly."

### TITLE NINE IRON

*No. 22 in the series*

**YEAR CREATED:** *2015*

**ISSUE:** *Women's equality in athletics*

**EDITION:** *143 prints; Zaharias won the first-ever women's Olympic javelin throw, with a distance of 143 feet*

**DONATION:** *Women's Sports Foundation*

It's not ENOUGH just TO

Swing at the BALL.

YOU'VE GOT TO Loosen YOUR girdle

AND Let 'er fly.

1
2
3

Babe DIDRIKSON ZAHARIAS

Mildred Ella "Babe" Didrikson Zaharias (1911 — 1956) grew up in Port Arthur, Texas. Babe reportedly earned her nickname playing baseball with neighborhood boys. She mastered every sport she played, including basketball, track and field, golf, tennis, diving, bowling, billiards and archery. When asked if there was anything she didn't play, Babe said, "Yeah, dolls."

In 1932, Didrikson entered an Amateur Athletic Union track and field championship as a one-woman team. She won six events, setting world records for the high jump, 80-meter hurdles, javelin and baseball throw. That same year, she won Olympic gold medals for the javelin and 80-meter hurdles and a silver medal in the high jump. Babe began playing golf in 1935, competing in the men's PGA tournament paired with golfer, pro wrestler and future husband George Zaharias. Over her career, Babe won an unprecedented 17 straight women's amateur victories and a total of 82 golf tournaments. A founding member of the Ladies Professional Golf Association, she was fiercely competitive and an entertainer on the course, challenging accepted notions of femininity and athleticism despite constant media scrutiny.

Babe was diagnosed with rectal cancer in 1953. A year after a colostomy, she won the U.S. Women's Open, inspiring cancer survivors with her victory. Golfer Betty Dodd played LPGA tours with Babe, eventually moving in with her and George for the last years of Babe's life. Their intimate relationship was never publicly acknowledged. Babe's cancer returned and she died at age 45. In 1999 the Associated Press named her Woman Athlete of the 20th Century.

Illustrated by Chandler O'Leary and printed by Jessica Spring, in honor of those who embrace their unique identities, "ladylike" or not. 143 copies were printed by hand at Springtide Press in Tacoma, during the U.S. Men's Open golf championship. June 2015.

# MARIE·CURIE

Born Marie Skłodowska on November 7, 1867, in Poland; studied at the Sorbonne in France ✦ Discovered the element polonium and named it after her home country ✦ Won the Nobel Prize twice, the first person and only woman ever to do so ✦ Died in 1934; first woman honored with burial in the Panthéon in Paris ✦ A unit of radioactivity is now known as a "curie"

Marie Skłodowska Curie approached play with the precision of a scientist—specifically through experimentation and the scientific method. Her "play" with the building blocks of matter made her a pioneer in the field of radioactivity—a term coined by Curie herself.

Born and raised in Russian-occupied Poland, Curie studied in secret at the Flying University, an underground institution that taught Polish students subjects that were opposed or banned by the controlling government. As laboratory study and higher education for women were illegal in Poland at the time, Curie immigrated to Paris to continue her studies. She met her husband, Pierre Curie, shortly afterward, and married him dressed in her dark blue laboratory outfit.

The Curies worked as collaborators until Pierre's death. Together they studied atomic radiation, isolating radioactive substances, and publishing groundbreaking papers. Curie's experiments, in particular, led to her discovery of two radioactive elements, which she named polonium and radium. Her papers on radium and cell destruction helped form the basis for modern cancer treatment.

Sadly, despite Curie's discoveries, the scientific community was yet unaware of the risks of prolonged exposure to radiation. After years of carrying test tubes in her pockets and working with x-rays without protective shields, Curie developed several chronic illnesses that led to her death. Even her personal effects and papers are dangerously radioactive and are kept today in lead-lined boxes.

◄ The Curies raised a family of scientists. Their daughter Iréne (pictured) and their grandchildren Hélène and Pierre became noted nuclear scientists in their own right.

▼ While the Curies experimented with radiation as a cure, students learned to "duck and cover" in the 1950s as part of drills in preparation for nuclear explosion.

◄ Curie declined to accept her first Nobel Prize in person because she was too busy working. Her second prize allowed her to persuade the French government to support her Radium Institute.

urie devoted her life (and ultimately her own health) to finding answers. She believed that "now is the time to understand more, so that we may fear less." Many of her experiments benefited the greater good, paving the way for new practices in medicine and providing effective new treatments for wounded soldiers in World War I. Yet unlike many of her contemporaries, Curie didn't seek to gain wealth or fame from her discoveries. She never sought a patent for her radium-isolation process, refused a number of awards, and gave away most of her Nobel Prize money to her friends, family, and colleagues. Her daughter Iréne inherited this philanthropic tendency, concealing her own work on nuclear fission to keep it out of military hands during World War II.

In stark contrast modern medicine is a multi-billion-dollar business these days. United States healthcare, including pharmaceuticals, is largely a for-profit industry. Even after the passage of the 2012 Affordable Care Act, many Americans risk bankruptcy due to illness or have to choose between food and life-saving medicines. We created our Curie broadside to add our voices to the debate over universal healthcare. Since the print was created, Americans have gained more freedom and security over healthcare, but the United States is still a long way from achieving a single-payer or universal system, and benefits vary wildly from state to state. As Curie would say: "One never notices what has been done; one can only see what remains to be done."

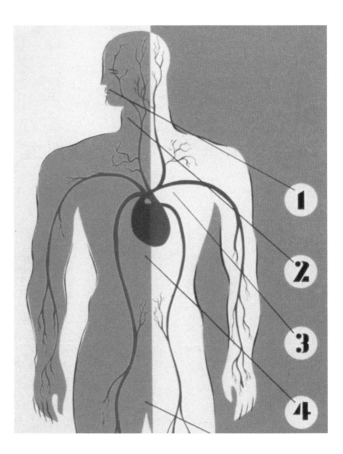

➤ Healthcare reform is still an ongoing debate in the United States. Currently the only state to pass single-payer healthcare legislation is Vermont, but the program was abandoned in 2014 due to cost restrictions.

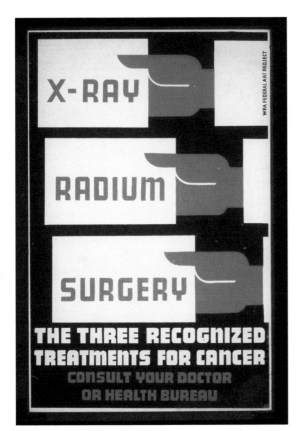

◄ The Works Progress Administration, a government agency formed during the Great Depression, created posters and pamphlets to raise public-health awareness.

▼ In 1921 President Harding presented Curie with a gram of radium to honor her founding of the Radium Institute. At the time, that gram would have cost over one hundred thousand dollars.

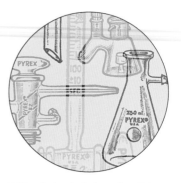

**1** Packaging from Radium Institute products inspired the hand-lettering on our broadside.

**2** Playful colors and graphics of midcentury chemistry illustrations informed *The Curie Cure.*

**3** The design includes a fanciful laboratory of connected equipment, representing the ripple effects made possible by political action.

**4** In the background is a pattern of atomic particles, arranged individually at the bottom of the page moving upward to form molecules.

**5** Just a few decades ago polonium was used in children's glow-in-the-dark toys, which produced a green light.

**6** We printed *The Curie Cure* with special fluorescent inks to represent the properties of radioactive elements.

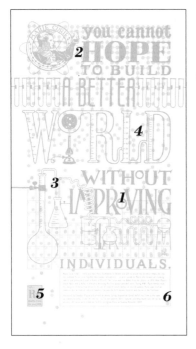

*"You cannot hope to build a better world without improving the individuals."*

## THE CURIE CURE

*No. 6 in the series*

**YEAR CREATED:** *2009*

**ISSUE:** *US healthcare reform and the universal healthcare movement*

**EDITION:** *138 prints; the half-life of polonium is 138 days*

**DONATION:** *No donations made this early in the series*

MARIE CURIE

you cannot **HOPE** TO BUILD A BETTER W✦RLD WITH✦UT IMPR✦VING THE INDIVIDUALS.

Marie Curie (1867 – 1934) was born Maria Sklodowska in Poland. She left to attend the Sorbonne where she met her husband Pierre Curie. Together they studied radioactivity — a term coined by Marie, who focused on isolating radium and polonium (named in honor of Poland). The Curies won the Nobel Prize for physics in 1903. After Pierre's death, Marie won a Nobel in chemistry, becoming the first person awarded twice. During WWI, Marie worked with her daughter Irene to train nurses in the use of xrays to locate bullets in injured soldiers. Marie later died of leukemia due to years of radiation exposure. She was the first woman honored with burial in the Pantheon.

Illustrated by Chandler O'Leary and printed by Jessica Spring, inspired by Curie's belief that "now is the time to understand more, so that we may fear less" as our country moves towards providing health care for all its citizens. 138 copies were printed by hand at Springtide Press in Tacoma. November 2009.

100%
**Rx**
Health Care
for everyONE

CHANDLER OLEARY               2/138

# SAPPHO

Born on the Greek island of Lesbos sometime between 630 and 612 BCE ✦ Most of
her poetry has been lost, though several fragments and one complete poem survive ✦
Poetry is characterized by colorful imagery and everyday moments ✦ Only woman
counted among the Nine Lyric Poets revered by ancient Greek culture ✦ Spent
part of her life in exile in Sicily and died in Greece, possibly around 570 BCE

Of all the feminists we have featured in our series, perhaps
the least is known about Sappho. In fact she is much more
readily associated with fable than with fact. So much myth,
half-truth, and downright falsehood have been written about
Sappho that it's difficult to catch a glimpse of the real woman
beneath it all.

We know that her wordplay and command of language
is legendary, but mostly we know this because there is
more surviving criticism *about* Sappho than text written *by*
Sappho. Plato called her the "tenth muse," praising her lyr-
icism and poetic imagery. She was frequently compared to
Homer and referred to as "the Poetess" (Homer was known
simply as "the Poet"). She often retold classic tales like
Homer's *Iliad*, reframing the stories from her own point
of view and focusing on intimate and domestic episodes
within the original works.

Our best source for details on Sappho's life is her own
writing, yet we'll never know for certain how much of her
work was autobiographical. In any case the fragments of
poetry that survive today paint vivid scenes of beauty and
art, love and loss, myth and metaphor. We may not know
much about Sappho as a person, but she certainly left us a
window into her mind.

◄ Sappho is depicted on this vase, circa 440 BCE, reading her poetry to a group of women. Historians have debated whether scenes like this one portray a student-teacher relationship or something more intimate. Regardless, physical passion is a central theme of her poetry; since the nineteenth century she has been a symbol of female homosexuality and eroticism.

▼ Famous figures of ancient Greece, both literary and mythic, are recurring characters in Sappho's work.

▲ Sappho was an object of fascination during the nineteenth century, and is represented by many works of art and literature from that time period.

I n 2004 another fragment of Sappho's poetry, called "Fragment 58," was discovered at the University of Cologne, Germany. The finding is significant because it lends new meaning to the body of Sappho poems that survive today. The new verses filled the gaps in an older, already known fragment, creating a new poem. "Fragment 58" focuses on old age, describing the loss of youth and the inevitability of change.

Sappho's use of metaphor here is both playful and mysterious. Some scholars see "Fragment 58" as a universal lament on growing old; others read it as a praise of beauty as a timeless gift independent of age. Either way the poem echoes the thoughts of every woman who struggles with her sense of self. For thousands of years women have been objects of both beauty and scorn, admiration and scrutiny—not just from society but from themselves as well.

We created our twenty-third broadside in both gratitude and frustration towards our own aging bodies. Like Sappho's so-called "Old Age Poem," body image is a play of both joy and sorrow. In hopes of bolstering the self-esteem of women of all ages, we donated a portion of our proceeds to About Face, an organization that helps women and girls resist the negative messages of popular culture.

▲ This fresco from ancient Pompeii is nicknamed "Sappho," but is more likely an intimate portrait of an ordinary woman. Still, the image is a fitting representation of Sappho in light of the discovery of "Fragment 58."

▲ Societal ideals of female beauty and body types have changed drastically through the ages, as evidenced by shifting tastes in fashion and the female silhouette.

▲ The actual papyrus text of "Fragment 58."

◄ On this vase, dated circa 470 BCE, Sappho is portrayed with the Aeolian poet Alcaeus, who called her "violethaired, pure, honey-smiling."

*1* Despite the more than two thousand years that have passed since Sappho wrote "Fragment 58," the poem reads like a modern diary entry.

*2* The colors and graphic style of our illustration are inspired by ancient Greek pottery, often adorned with narrative or allegorical scenes.

*3* Layers of thin paper or "makeready" are used on the press to assist with both large floods of ink and a delicate colophon.

*4* Hidden in the design are references to classical Greek characters, in homage to similar cameos that appear in Sappho's works.

*5* The typography references ancient Greek inscriptions.

*6* Nobody knows what Sappho looked like for certain, but the description of the woman in her "Old Age Poem" is both specific and universal.

## "To be human is to grow old."

—From "Fragment 58" (as translated by Josephine Balmer)

### AGE BEFORE BEAUTY

*No. 23 in the series*

**YEAR CREATED:** *2015*

**ISSUE:** *Body image and aging*

**EDITION:** *158; fifty-eight for "Fragment 58" plus one hundred*

**DONATION:** *About Face*

*to be* HUMAN

IS TO GROW OLD.

Sappho

Sappho (c. 630 – 570 BCE) is the only woman counted among the Nine Lyric Poets revered in ancient Greek culture. Plato called her "the tenth muse," but all that remains of her work is a handful of fragments. This quote is an excerpt from Fragment 58, a mysterious *Old Age Poem* that can be read either as a lament or a celebration of mortality. Illustrated by Chandler O'Leary and printed by Jessica Spring, in hopes that all women might see themselves both with Aphrodite's gaze and Athena's wisdom. 158 COPIES WERE PRINTED BY HAND AT SPRINGTIDE PRESS IN TACOMA, FEBRUARY 2016

CHANDLER O'LEARY                    5/158

# CHAPTER 8

*Share*

These women didn't share much in common, but each staked her claim on history. One demanded equal stakes for all—and shared the title of America's Most Wanted. Another was a Founding Mother, sharing the story of a young country through a lifetime of letters. The third was the last monarch of her people, forced to share her country with foreign colonists.

# Emma Goldman

Born June 27, 1869; moved to New York in 1885 ✦ News of the Chicago Haymarket Riot inspired her to devote her life to political causes ✦ Founded the *Mother Earth* journal as a platform for anarchism and the principle of absolute freedom ✦ Arrested numerous times for inciting to riot and disseminating illegal information ✦ Died in 1940; buried near Haymarket Square

Emma Goldman was born in Kovno, then part of the Russian Empire (now Kaunas, Lithuania)—a city that throughout its history has been conquered, occupied, and ruled by foreign powers many times over. Perhaps this fact influenced Goldman's reaction to the Chicago Haymarket Square labor riot that rocked her adopted country, the United States, in 1886. The event inflamed her sympathies for workers' rights into a militant passion for freedom at any cost.

Shortly afterward Goldman met prominent anarchist, future lover, and fellow Russian immigrant Alexander Berkman. From Berkman she learned the basics of public speaking, and quickly began a career of political activism. She spoke and wrote on the topics of labor unions, unemployment, equal pay for women, birth control, and a variety of anarchist causes. Goldman was an outspoken proponent of total freedom for both sexes: economic, sexual, political, and otherwise.

Emma's beliefs and actions frequently landed her in trouble. She was jailed many times: for inciting workers to riot, for disseminating illegal birth control information, even for conspiracy to commit murder. During World War I her public opposition to the passage of the Selective Service Act finally gave authorities the chance they were looking for. J. Edgar Hoover called her and Berkman "the most dangerous anarchists in this country"; he was determined to make the charges stick. After serving fourteen months in prison, Emma was deported back to Russia under the 1918 Alien Act.

Goldman continued to campaign in exile, right up until her death in 1940. Her body was repatriated to the United States and interred outside of Chicago—near the graves of the executed anarchist Haymarket rioters that inspired her life's work.

NING, SEPTEMBER 22, 1901.

EMMA
GOLDMAN

◄ While she was eventually cleared of the charges, Goldman's rhetoric implicated her in the assassination of President William McKinley.

▼ Goldman's support for laborers, coupled with her hatred of capitalism, brought some of her beliefs in line with her communist contemporaries in Russia.

◄ Although she was not a witness to the event, Goldman felt a strong connection to the Haymarket Riot. She dedicated her work "to the memory of [her] martyred comrades, to make their cause [her] own."

oldman is a controversial figure—and choosing to feature her in our series proved problematic. Her political views were so far outside the mainstream that even today her words and deeds garner suspicion. She believed in communal causes like shared property, but her refusal to compromise made her the very antithesis of a team player. Thanks to her support of targeted political violence, her disdain for religion, and her view of democracy as fascism "in disguise," she made enemies everywhere. Her lack of support for women's suffrage especially—which she saw as a distraction, with government itself the real enemy—makes her, in our eyes, a less than ideal symbol for feminism.

Despite all this her views on love and sexual freedom were revolutionary. In an era when even her fellow anarchists questioned her support of homosexuality, Goldman's words were empathetic and nuanced: "It is a tragedy, I feel, that people of different sexual type are caught in a world which shows so little understanding . . . and is so crassly indifferent to the various gradations and variations of gender." Whatever else she might have been, she understood that people—and relationships—come in all shapes, sizes, and shades.

Goldman spent her entire life fighting for the acceptance of outsiders and the triumph of personal liberty. Since her thoughts on love cut straight to the heart of the matter, we found her to be a perfect voice for marriage equality. Sometimes it takes an anarchist to bring a struggle to order.

▲ Goldman frequently justified the use of violence as a means to an end. This stance is problematic in light of the struggle for LGBTQ equality considering the many gay, transgender, and queer victims of violence.

◄ Goldman saw all relationships as a shared commitment between equals: "I demand the independence of woman . . . to love whomever she pleases, or as many as she pleases. I demand freedom for both sexes, freedom of action, freedom in love, and freedom in motherhood."

▼ We shared our donation between two organizations close to our hearts. Tacoma's Rainbow Center is dedicated to eliminating discrimination based on sexual orientation and gender. Oasis Youth Center provides support for LGBTQ teens and youth.

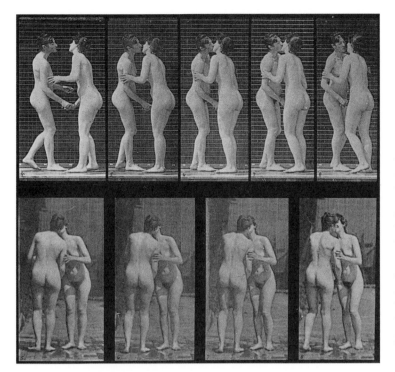

◄ Goldman's support of same-sex, poly-amorous, and other types of relationships is refreshingly inclusive. Her outspoken views predated the free-love sentiments associated with hippies by nearly half a century.

*1* Each color requires a separate plate and pass through the press, which when registered can create additional colors.

*2* We made *matryoshka* dolls the focal point of our broadside to represent the diversity nested within every family.

*3* The floral motifs in the design represent Goldman's Russian heritage.

*4* Historic floriated typography inspired the folksy lettering in *Love Nest*.

*5* In honor of Goldman's subversive rhetoric, we included a very modern brood of chicks. The word "love" adds a subtle twist on traditional homespun motifs.

*6* Our gender-bending nesting dolls create a tongue-in-cheek play on contemporary hip-folk culture.

*"The most vital right is the right to love and be loved."*

## LOVE NEST

*No. 15 in the series*

**YEAR CREATED:** *2012*

**ISSUE:** *Marriage equality and families of every shape and color*

**EDITION:** *126 prints; number of years (at the time of printing) since the Chicago Haymarket Riot that inspired Goldman's work*

**DONATION:** *Rainbow Center and Oasis Youth Center*

the ✦ most VITAL RIGHT is the right to LOVE and be loved.

emma goldman

Emma Goldman (1869–1940) was born in Kovno, part of the Russian Empire (now Lithuania). She moved to New York in 1885 to live with relatives, supporting herself with factory work. In the following year, news of the Chicago Haymarket riot changed Goldman's life. In honor of the riot victims and the labor movement, she determined to "dedicate myself to the memory of my martyred comrades, to make their cause my own." She joined Alexander Berkman — another Russian immigrant — in spreading her vision of an ideal society, based on the anarchist principle of absolute freedom. Goldman founded the political and literary journal *Mother Earth*, and toured the country speaking about anarchism, birth control and economic freedom for women. She was arrested numerous times over her unconventional opinions, accused of disseminating illegal information and inciting to riot.

At a time when even her fellow anarchists questioned her support of homosexuality, Goldman spoke out: "It is a tragedy, I feel, that people of different sexual type are caught in a world which shows so little understanding ... and is so crassly indifferent to the various gradations and variations of gender." She openly opposed U.S. entry into WWI, was jailed once more for obstruction of the draft, and finally deported back to Russia under the 1918 Alien Act. She spent the rest of her life in exile, supporting anarchist causes abroad. After her death, Goldman's body was repatriated and buried in Chicago — near the Haymarket anarchists that had so inspired her.

Illustrated by Chandler O'Leary and printed by Jessica Spring, who with Goldman "demand freedom for both sexes, freedom of action, freedom in love and freedom in motherhood." 126 copies were printed by hand at Springtide Press in Tacoma. June 2012

CHANDLER O'LEARY                    1/126

# Jane Mecom

Born Jane Franklin in 1712 in Boston, the youngest daughter of a soap maker ✦ Married saddler Edward Mecom at the age of fifteen ✦ Corresponded with brother Benjamin Franklin for most of her life, though all letters written before 1758 are lost ✦ Escaped the Revolutionary War in 1775 by fleeing to Rhode Island ✦ Died in 1794, after outliving nearly everyone in her family

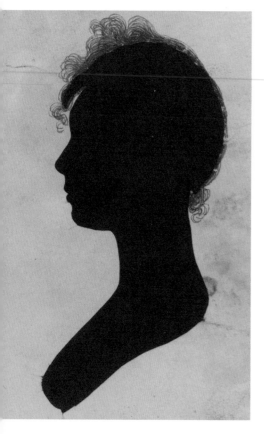

*Signed, Sealed, Soapbox* is the first Dead Feminists broadside to feature two historical figures—and the only piece where a man makes a cameo. Our leading lady is known thanks to her famous brother Benjamin Franklin—so we decided to highlight his life as well, to give context to hers.

There are few Founding Fathers more famous than Franklin, but Jane Mecom* was something of a mystery. Her life was marked with misfortune, poverty, and the deaths of nearly everyone she loved. By running both the family soap-making trade and a boarding house, Mecom supported twelve children and a husband unable to work. Sadly she outlived all but one child, and documented the tragedies that befell her loved ones in her *Book of Ages*—a journal that lists the deaths of everyone she loved.

Mecom's correspondence with her brother gives us the best glimpse of her life and personality. Despite being barely literate, she craved knowledge. "I read as much as I dare," she said, devouring her brother's letters and political papers. Franklin wrote more letters to Mecom than to any other person in his life—including his fellow statesmen. He called her his "peculiar favorite" and even sought her opinion on his essay drafts. In return Mecom revered him above all others in her life. On his eighty-fourth birthday she wrote of Franklin: "Who that know and love you can bear the thoughts of surviving you in this gloomy world?"

History has practically forgotten Jane Franklin Mecom, but her brother never did. Franklin provided for her both in life and after his death. "My dear brother supplied all," his sister once wrote. Meanwhile, Mecom provided us with her valuable insight and an intimate portrait of one of our greatest leaders.

---

* No surviving portraits of Mecom exist to our knowledge. This is an historic cut-paper silhouette.

➤ Girls' education in the colonial period was generally limited to basic reading. Stitched samplers like this one were a popular pursuit and may have been an effective tool for learning the alphabet.

▼ While formal apprenticeships were not available to girls and women, Mecom was the most skilled maker of her family's Crown Soap. Franklin accused other family members of making and selling inferior soap.

▲ While none of Boston's historical markers mention Mecom by name, she was well-known in her time as a businesswoman and Franklin's sister. Notable figures of the day paid their respects in deference to Franklin.

◄ Franklin had just two years of formal schooling, but later earned honorary degrees from Harvard, Yale, and Oxford. His poor background taught him to value hard work, thrift, charity, education, and tolerance.

*E*very girl in America grows up learning the stories of the Founding Fathers in school—if she's lucky, a few Founding Mothers (Betsy Ross, Martha Washington, Abigail Adams) make it into her education as well. Yet on the whole the lives of early American women are simply absent from the history books.

We stumbled upon the story of Mecom thanks to a 2011 *New York Times* article by Jill Lepore (who graciously wrote the foreword to this book). Her essay—which she later expanded into a book—tells the tale of two siblings, whose destinies are predetermined by their respective genders. Mecom's life is one of poverty, ignorance, and endless babies, while her brother's exploits and opportunities earned him a fortune and helped build a nation.

Yet while Franklin shaped his young country with rhetoric and diplomacy, Mecom also left her mark on history—albeit in smaller ways. As a skilled craftswoman and entrepreneur, she contributed to a growing national economy. She shared her trade secrets and soap recipe with younger makers, thus continuing the lineage of her family's profession. And she was a key witness of the American Revolution—first from her boarding house in British-occupied Boston, then later as a war refugee on a Rhode Island farm, and finally as her brother's guest in newly independent Philadelphia. Few ordinary women of her time would have been so well traveled or had such insight into the leadership of their young country. It is the generous nature of her relationship with her brother that granted her these experiences—and which by extension shared with us this rare window into early American life.

➤ Franklin was a self-made man and also a generous one. He provided decades of financial support for Mecom, and upon his death bequeathed public education trusts to Boston and Philadelphia.

▲ We released our broadside at the height of the occupy Wall Street movement, inspired by Franklin's wise words: "Yes, we must, indeed, all hang together, or most assuredly we shall all hang separately."

◄ Mecom and Franklin had the ideal sibling relationship. In their honor we donated to Big Brothers Big Sisters—which provides children facing adversity with mentors who change their lives for the better.

▲ The Pulitzer Prize rewards achievements in journalism with a medal portraying Franklin and a handpress. In addition to being inspired by his words and deeds, we feel an affinity to Franklin as a printer.

*1* The broadside features a colonial blue reminiscent of the famous matte glazes of Wedgwood ceramics.

*2* The dialogue portion of our design replicates Mecom's and Franklin's actual handwriting.

*3* Our broadside is a love letter to correspondence, inspired by Franklin's role as the first post-master general of the United States.

*4* Though there is no surviving likeness of Jane Mecom, we looked to *The Comtesse d'Haussonville* by French painter Jean-Auguste-Dominique Ingres.

*5* Colonial paperwork is characterized by the curves and ornate details of penmanship. Our design revives this fading art form with a bold copperplate script.

*6* The ornate scenes of toile patterns dominated the fabrics and wall-papers of the eighteenth century, and inspired the birds-and-branches motif of our design.

*"My power was allways small tho my will is good."*—JANE MECOM

*"Energy and persistence conquer all things."* —BENJAMIN FRANKLIN

## SIGNED, SEALED, SOAPBOX

*No. 14 in the series*

**YEAR CREATED:** *2011*

**ISSUE:** *Education equality; the value of mentorship; the Occupy Wall Street movement*

**EDITION:** *176 prints; America declared independence from England in 1776*

**DONATION:** *Big Brothers Big Sisters*

My power was Allways small

Tho my will is Good.

Energy and Persistence Conquer all Things.

I have wrote & spelt this very badly but as it is to Won who I am sure will make all Reasonable allowances for me and not let any won Els see it I shall venter to send it & subscrib my self yr Ever affecti onat Sister,

**JANE MECOM.**

Is there not a little Affectation in your Apology for the Incorrectness of your Writing? Perhaps it is rather too much for Commendation. You write better, in my Opinion, than most American Women. Believe me ever Your loving Brother

**B FRANKLIN.**

Jane (Franklin) Mecom (1712–1794) was born in Boston's North End, the youngest daughter of a soap maker. Married at fifteen, she had no formal education but was a voracious reader of books supplied by her brother. She ran a boarding house and made soap to support her ailing husband, her elderly parents, and twelve children. She outlived all but one of them. Her "Book of Ages" chronicles the deaths of these loved ones, but what little we know of Jane herself can be traced to a lifetime correspondence with her beloved brother.

Benjamin Franklin (1706–1790) attended school for just two years before becoming a printer's apprentice at age twelve, but was eventually awarded honorary degrees from Harvard, Yale and Oxford. He founded the first lending library in America, reformed the colonial postal system and became the first U.S. Postmaster General. He espoused the values of thrift, hard work, education, community spirit and tolerance, and opposed authoritarianism in both religion and politics.

Despite the differences in their education and circumstances, Benjamin largely treated his sister as an equal, and penned more letters to her than any other person in his life. He sent his writings and political essays to get Jane's opinion, and notable figures of the day visited her to pay their respects out of deference to the famous Franklin. Benjamin provided decades of financial support for Jane and her children, and upon his death bequeathed her a comfortable living — as well as public trusts to the cities of Boston and Philadelphia to fund mortgages, school scholarships and eventually establish the Franklin Institute of Technology.

Illustrated by Chandler O'Leary and printed by Jessica Spring, 100% occupied with Benjamin's wise words — and deeds — as he signed the Declaration of Independence: "Yes, we must, indeed, all hang together, or most assuredly we shall all hang separately." 176 copies were printed by hand at Springtide Press in Tacoma. November 2011

CHANDLER O'LEARY

106/176

# Lili'uokalani

Born Lydia Lili'u Loloku Walania Wewehi Kamaka'eha on September 2, 1838 ✦ Elected heir apparent to the Kingdom of Hawai'i in 1877 ✦ Attempted to restore voting rights to Native Hawaiians ✦ Deposed by foreign businessmen after less than two years on the throne ✦ Spent eight months under house arrest, and afterward was forbidden to leave the island of O'ahu ✦ Worked to preserve traditional Hawaiian culture until her death in 1917

Queen Lili'uokalani was the last monarch—and only queen regnant—of the Kingdom of Hawai'i. She grew up in a colonized nation, where two cultures had a role in shaping her future. Her reign was sadly brief—thanks to powerful foreign interests who refused to share the nation they had claimed for their own.

Lili'uokalani learned the value of sharing and cooperation from an early age. Born to the royal family, she was raised the *hānai* (adopted) child of High Chief Abner Pākī and his wife. *Hānai* was a Hawaiian tradition practiced by noble and common families alike—sharing children with parents unable to produce heirs of their own, in order to strengthen family ties. Perhaps this concept of a broader human family had a role in her commitment to nonviolence and attempts at negotiation with her enemies.

She ascended the throne in 1891, after the death of her brother. Yet almost immediately, white sugar growers and businessmen plotted an overthrow of the monarchy, fearing a loss of revenue from a series of proposed changes to the Constitution that sought to benefit Native Hawaiians. With the help of the US Marines, the conspirators worked quickly, smoothly deposing Lili'uokalani in January of 1893. Just five years later, without due constitutional process, Hawai'i was annexed to the United States by President McKinley—the same president in whose assassination Emma Goldman was implicated. In 1959 Hawai'i became the fiftieth US state.

Lili'uokalani died in 1917, but she is remembered for far more than her reign alone. She was also a talented writer, singer, and multi-instrument musician. She was the first Native Hawaiian female author, and composed over 150 songs, many of which have become anthems of Hawaiian culture.

▲ Lili'uokalani's throne was usurped by Hawai'i-born American Sanford B. Dole, named president of the new Republic of Hawai'i. Dole's cousin James was one of several American plantation owners who benefited from annexation.

The House of Representatives of the United States:

I, Liliuokalani of Hawaii, named heir apparent on the 10th day of April, 1877, and proclaimed queen of the Hawaiian Islands on the 29th day of January, 1891, do hereby, protest against the assertion of ownership by the United States of America of the so-called Hawaiian Crown Lands amounting to about one million acres and which are my property, and I especially protest against such assertion of ownership as a taking of property without due process of law and without just or other compensation.

Therefore, supplementing my protest of June 17, 1897, I call upon the President and the National Legislature and the People of the United States to do justice in this matter and to restore to me this property, the enjoyment of which is being withheld from me by your Government under what must be a misapprehension of my right and title.

Done at Washington, District of Columbia, United States of America, this nineteenth day of December, in the year one thousand eight hundred and ninety-eight.

Witness
J. H. Douglass

Liliuokalani

▲ Aside from her reign, Lili'uokalani's most famous legacy may be her music. A prolific composer of traditional Hawaiian music, her best-known song, "Aloha 'Oe" has become a cultural symbol of Hawai'i.

◄ Unlike militant feminists like Emma Goldman, Lili'uokalani was staunchly nonviolent. Her statement that surrendered her royal authority included an eloquent protest to the overthrow of her government.

*L*iliʻuokalani's story shares common themes with those of colonized peoples throughout the world. For centuries white colonial powers imposed their rule and customs upon every Indigenous culture they encountered—and expected the people to conform or face punishment, imprisonment, and warfare.

Like Indigenous women around the globe, Hawaiian women saw their rights and status decrease with the imposition of white culture. Liliʻuokalani believed her deposition was hastened by the distaste American businessmen expressed for a female head of state. Yet she did not come to power by line of automatic succession. Though she was born royal and named heir by her brother Kalākaua, Hawaiʻi's Constitutional Monarchy required her to be elected before she could assume the throne. If Hawaiʻi had somehow managed to retain its monarchy beyond 1893, it's unlikely the colonial powers would have allowed the election of another queen—even though Victoria was on the English throne at the time.

Before first contact with the West, Hawaiʻi was a matriarchal society. A family's lineage was traced through the maternal line, and genealogical records were kept by oral tradition. Most people had just one name; the concept of surnames wasn't introduced until white settlement. During Liliʻuokalani's imprisonment, she was forced to add her husband's last name to her signature. This infuriated her: "There is not, and never was . . . any such a person as Liliʻuokalani Dominis."

Still, Liliʻuokalani lived in both Hawaiian and white cultures, and was fluent in the customs and languages of each. She dressed in Western clothing and wore Victorian hairstyles, but she worked tirelessly to preserve and promote traditional Hawaiian art forms like *mele* (chants or songs) and the hula. For Indigenous women like Liliʻuokalani, there is no going back to life before Euro-American contact. Yet by sharing their traditions with future generations, they have helped create a path forward.

▲ A hundred years after the overthrow of the Kingdom of Hawaiʻi, the United States issued a formal apology to Native Hawaiians. Meanwhile, there is still a strong pro-secession movement.

◄ Hawaiian culture is now a major draw for the millions of tourists who visit the islands. The impact of tourism to both the cultural and natural environments of the islands remains an ongoing challenge.

▼ Indigenous women have been objects of curiosity to Westerners since the colonial era. One of the most famous is the stereotypical hula girl, an icon appropriated from traditional Hawaiian culture.

◄ Thanks to the second Hawaiian renaissance, which began in 1970, Hawai'i has seen a resurgence in its traditional customs. Many art forms, like hula, have seen a return to their authentic roots.

# TAKE A CLOSER LOOK AT *SONG OF ALOHA*

**1** Some of the shapes and motifs in our design are reminiscent of traditional Hawaiian appliqué quilts.

**2** As a symbol of the vanished Hawaiian monarchy, every bird in the design is an extinct Hawaiian species.

**3** The tropical flora and fauna required mixing a multitude of bright inks.

**4** Yellow is a dominant color in the piece, as it was the symbolic color of Queen Lili'uokalani's reign.

**5** 'Iolani Palace was the royal residence until the end of Queen Lili'uokalani's reign. It was used as the capitol building until 1969.

**6** Hidden in the design is a line of music from Lili'uokalani's famous composition, "Aloha 'Oe."

# "E onipa'a . . . i ka'imi na'auao" (Be steadfast in the seeking of knowledge)

## SONG OF ALOHA

*No. 24 in the series*

**YEAR CREATED:** *2016*

**ISSUE:** *The shared responsibility for protecting our communities and the environment*

**EDITION:** *192 prints; this is our twenty-fourth broadside, and Lili'uokalani was the eighth and final monarch of the Kingdom of Hawai'i; 24 x 8 = 192*

**DONATION:** *This broadside marks the inauguration of the Dead Feminists Foundation*

Be steadfast IN THE Seeking of knowledge.

E' onipa'a... i ka 'imi na 'auao.

QUEEN LILI'UOKALANI

Lili'uokalani (1838 – 1917) was the last monarch and only queen regnant of the Kingdom of Hawai'i. Born into the royal family, she ascended the throne in 1891 via traditional election after the death of her brother. She reigned for less than two years, until Sanford B. Dole — backed by American business interests and the Marines — deposed her and dismantled the monarchy. Dole placed Lili'uokalani under house arrest and despite her formal letters of protest, Hawai'i was annexed by the United States in 1898 without due constitutional process.

Queen Lili'uokalani lived with one foot planted in each culture, embracing Victorian dress and Western mannerisms while working tirelessly to preserve traditional Hawaiian art forms. A prolific singer, musician and composer, her best known song was "Aloha 'Oe" ("Farewell to Thee"), written in both Hawaiian and English.

Illustrated by Chandler O'Leary and printed by Jessica Spring, knowing that the spirit of aloha can honor what we've lost and save what remains. 192 copies were printed by hand at Springtide Press in Tacoma. October 2016

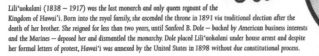

THANDLER O'LEARY                24/192

Afterword

Engage

# ENGAGING WITH OUR AUDIENCE

When we began the Dead Feminists series, we hoped to make a contribution for the record—to actively engage with politics, rather than simply consuming the news or discussing current events. What we didn't expect was for others to engage *with* us, by responding to what we created. In the years since we started, we've been introduced to an entire community of living feminists—an active and passionate audience that has helped give the series a life of its own.

When we first started releasing broadsides, they existed simply as limited-edition posters, printed in small batches and collected by fellow artists and whoever happened to stumble upon them online or at our events. But almost immediately, those collectors started spreading the word, bringing our work to the attention of their friends, colleagues, students, and children. Most of them were women, and many of them were students—the next generation of feminists.

▲ Chandler (left) and Jessica at Springtide Press.

▼ The annual Tacoma Wayzgoose festival has helped bring the Dead Feminists to a wider audience within our own community. Each year we create a huge steamroller print that relates to our series.

Before long we started using the Dead Feminists series as a platform in its own right. We began giving lectures about the series, writing blog posts and articles about the women we featured, and making donations with each new piece. Teachers and librarians who collected our work told us they were using our broadsides in the classroom, as teaching aids for everything from English and graphic design to history and women's studies. The editions sold out more and more quickly, and we began releasing reproduction postcards to keep up with the demand and provide a low-cost format for our imagery. Museums, universities, and libraries added our broadsides to their permanent collections, allowing the prints to be seen by a larger community. Along with the historical women we featured, we had a place in political culture, and tangible evidence of the power of the press (even today).

▲ The University of Washington Libraries and the University of Puget Sound are two of the institutions that have collected our entire series to date. Both collections are open to the public by appointment, making our broadsides permanently accessible to anyone, free of charge.

## ENGAGING IN DIALOGUE

By combining historical quotes with modern issues using old-school printing techniques, we wanted our series to engage in a dialogue with the past and present. Researching these women's lives and time periods gave us a chance to get inside their heads for a bit and breathe new life into words spoken and written long ago.

Of course this approach is somewhat problematic. For one thing, we're intentionally taking each quote out of context, plucking each feminist out of her era, and attempting to fit her into our own framework. In the light of the modern day, some of the women we've featured are glaringly out of place. Many of them employed ideas and rhetoric that would be considered racist, insensitive, or simply outdated today. Others have largely disappeared from the historical record, leaving us to fill in the blanks with projection and guesswork. And above all, we're not historians or feminist scholars. We're simply artists with opinions and biases like anybody else. Our series is our take on current events, based on our fascination with the past.

Still, the response to our work tells us that it's better to engage imperfectly than not to engage at all. We've done our best to create a diverse mix of featured feminists, from famous icons to obscure figures, representatives of our own culture and women from a variety of racial and cultural backgrounds. We've highlighted women who would never have considered themselves feminists, or who might have disagreed with our own opinions on various political issues. Taken together, the result is a motley crew of ladies who, if they had actually gathered together in a room, probably would have argued bitterly with one another. Yet that's part of what keeps us going with the series: the idea of placing these women in a modern context and wondering what might happen.

## STAYING ENGAGED

By featuring a wide variety of issues and representing many different styles and motifs, we've been able to bring feminism to a broader audience than we ever could have imagined at the start of our series. Yet it feels as if we've hardly begun, and that we're still mainly preaching to the choir. For example, we still get asked all the time if we'd ever consider featuring any historical men—even though the name of our series makes our intent pretty clear. We haven't quite figured out a

diplomatic response to that one, but one of our lecture attendees had a snappy rejoinder: "Want to read quotes by dead men? Open a book some time."

What this indicates to us is a pressing need for women's voices in political dialogue. We're reminded again and again that we're still fighting the battles that our foremothers fought generations ago—proof that the words of women who died long ago are still pertinent today, and that despite whole lifetimes many of them devoted to various causes, we aren't done yet. Most heartening of all are the words of all the living feminists we've met—they tell us that people are still listening. It has shown us that whatever changes come to technology and society, the centuries-old medium of the broadside continues to be relevant.

Still, we feel we have a long way to go—and many more broadsides in our future. There are still many holes in our series: many feminist issues we haven't yet covered—like reproductive and transgender rights—and a long wish list of women we'd like to feature. And every day, it seems, there's some new crisis to cover, some new battle to fight. As the old adage says, a woman's work is never done.

▲ Dead Feminists broadsides on display at Springtide Press, Jessica's print shop.

# Acknowledgments

❖ ❖ ❖

**CHANDLER AND JESSICA:** When we launched the Dead Feminists, our subscribers had no idea they'd be signing up for the long haul. Their enthusiasm and commitment helped *build* the foundation of our series, and inspire us to continue. Gallerists and dealers who represent us, like Bill and Vicky Stewart, Sweet Pea Flaherty, Wessel & Lieberman, and Laura Russell, allowed us to *grow*. Institutions that collect our broadsides *protect* our work for future generations; thanks to Jane Carlin, Sandra Kroupa, Danelle Moon, Molly Dotson, and Heather Slania. Our research led us to *collaborate* with filmmaker Nancy Bourne Haley and book artist Allison Milham. Without the sharp proofreader's eye of Ric Matthies, supplies from Boxcar Press, and advice from Susan Estelle Kwas and Laurie Cinotto, we'd never be able to *make* broadsides or this book. Ladies of Letterpress founders Kseniya Thomas and Jessica C. White gave us the chance to *engage*, first at their inaugural conference, then through their book. Educators and writers who *tell* their students and readers about our work challenge us to find the next story. Amy McBride and Naomi Strom-Avila gave us room to *play* in Tacoma. Jill Lepore *led* the way with her scholarship and encouragement. And our editor Hannah Elnan, along with her team at Sasquatch Books, gave us the opportunity to *share* our story with you.

**CHANDLER:** Being an artist can feel like a solitary business at times—yet I am surrounded by friends, mentors, and supporters, all of whom have made this book possible. I owe many thanks to Regula Russelle and Paulette Myers-Rich, the women who taught me to print, and to David Macaulay and Michael O'Leary, the men who taught me to tell a story. To Charlie Quimby and Jeff Rathermel, who each took a chance on me and opened the door to a new world. To Sarah Christianson, my second pair of eyes; Mary-Alice Pomputius, my right-hand gal; and Elizabeth Anderson, whose ears and heart I treasure. To my family, for cheering me on, and to my husband, Donald Sidman, for being the embodiment of the expression "better half." Most of all, to Jessica Spring, for being my partner in crime, my dear friend, my gossip girl, and the one with all the best ideas. I am forever grateful.

**JESSICA:** Letterpress printers have an incredible community, one that is generous, inclusive, and fiercely protective of a craft we all care so much about preserving. I have been fortunate to spend a lifetime among these crazy, funny people—especially members of the Amalgamated Printers' Association and a long list of beloved Springtide Press stalwarts who have kept the shop humming—thank you all, especially Gabby Cooksey and Taylor Cox. There is no way I'd be printing if my sweet husband, Tim Allen, didn't cheerfully agree to "just one more" equipment move or crazy deadline. Our son, Jack, has been roped into many printing adventures—hopefully he'll catch the bug. Finally, for Chandler, who constantly amazes me with her magic drawing and writing superpowers bundled with boundless energy. Thank you for bringing me along: what fun we've had!

# Learn More

❖ ❖ ❖

## BOOKS, FILMS, AND WEBSITES

*Bad Feminist* by Roxane Gay

*Book of Ages: The Life and Opinions of Jane Franklin* by Jill Lepore

*Chisholm '72: Unbought and Unbossed*, a documentary film by Shola Lynch

*Finding Thea*, a documentary film by Nancy Bourne Haley and Lucy Ostrander

*Ladies of Letterpress* by Kseniya Thomas and Jessica C. White

LadiesOfLetterpress.com

LadyPartsJustice.com

*Men Explain Things to Me* by Rebecca Solnit

*Rad Women A-Z* by Kate Schatz and Miriam Klein Stahl

*The Secret History of Wonder Woman* by Jill Lepore

## PERMANENT COLLECTIONS WHERE YOU CAN FIND THE DEAD FEMINISTS

Baylor University (Moody Memorial Library), Waco, TX

Claremont Colleges, Claremont, CA

Denison University (Doane Library), Granville, OH

George Mason University (Fenwick Library), Fairfax, VA

International Printing Museum (Prints Collection), Carson, CA

Multnomah County Library (Wilson Special Collections), Portland, OR

National Museum of Women in the Arts, Washington, DC

Northwestern University (Deering Library Special Collections), Evanston, IL

Nova Southeastern University (Farquhar College), Fort Lauderdale, FL

Occidental College (Clapp Library), Los Angeles, CA

Radcliffe Institute (Schlesinger Library), Cambridge, MA

San Diego State University (Special Collections), San Diego, CA

San Jose State University (King Library), San Jose, CA

Stanford University (Bowes Art and Architecture Library), Stanford, CA

Topeka and Shawnee County Public Library, Topeka, KS

University of California, Santa Barbara (Davidson Library Special Collections), Santa Barbara, CA

University of Puget Sound (Collins Memorial Library), Tacoma, WA

University of Washington Libraries (Book Arts Collection), Seattle, WA

Washington State Library (Special Collections), Tumwater, WA

Yale University (Haas Arts Library Special Collections), New Haven, CT

# Image Credits

❖ ❖ ❖

A Jewish woman does embroidery next to a sewing machine in a workshop in Łódź Ghetto, c. 1940 to 1944. Courtesy of the United States Holocaust Memorial Museum, 454.15585. Used with permission: page 98

A young writer at 826CHI, Chicago, Illinois. Courtesy of 826Chi. Used with permission: page 27 (top left)

Adina De Zavala, c. 1908. Courtesy of the University of Texas at San Antonio Libraries Special Collections. Used with permission: page 58

American writer Gwendolyn Brooks, of Chicago, Ill., poses with her first book of poems titled "A Street in Bronzeville," 1945, in this undated photo at an unknown location. Brooks was awarded the 1950 Pulitzer Prize for poetry for "Annie Allen," 1949, becoming the first African American writer to win the Pulitzer Prize. (AP Photo). ©2016 Associated Press. Used under AP editorial license: page 24

Annie Oakley and Frank Butler, 1925. Courtesy of Buffalo Bill Center of the West, P.6.339. Used with permission: page 53 (bottom right)

Annie Oakley shooting with other women, c. 1920. Courtesy of Buffalo Bill Center of the West, P.69.1177. Used with permission: page 54

Anti-Chinese agitation in Seattle, Washington, as illustrated in West Shore, March 1886. Courtesy of University of Washington Libraries, PH Coll 1293. Used with permission: page 61 (top)

Arabic manuscript on medicine and pharmacology, c. 1612. Courtesy of the Cushing/Whitney Medical Library, Yale University: page 19 (top left)

Bernice Sapp working at the Washington State supreme court, 1914. Courtesy of the Washington State Historical Society. Used with permission: page 119 (top left)

Courtesy of Chandler O'Leary's ephemera collection: pages 22 (bottom right), 59 (bottom), 62 (bottom right), 86, 102 (top right), 128 (top left), 141 (bottom left), 142 (bottom left), 162 (top right and bottom right), 165 (bottom right), 166, 167 (bottom right), 168 (bottom right)

Courtesy of Google Book Search's digitized collection of public-domain books: page 116 (bottom left)

Courtesy of Google Images, public domain info courtesy of Wikimedia Commons: page 78

Courtesy of Jessica Spring's ephemera collection: pages 5 (bottom), 15 (bottom right), 25 (top left), 33 (top right and bottom left), 34, 35 (bottom right), 36 (top right), 47 (top right), 55 (bottom), 56 (top middle), 56 (bottom right), 59 (middle), 61 (bottom), 65 (bottom left), 67 (bottom right), 75 (all), 81 (top right), 96 (bottom right), 122 (top left), 122 (bottom left), 125 (top right), 126, 127 (bottom left), 128 (bottom left), 133 (bottom left), 135 (bottom), 136 (bottom middle), 142 (top middle), 153 (bottom right), 155 (bottom left and right), 168 (bottom middle)

Courtesy of Library of Congress: pages 3, 12, 13, 14, 15 (top right and bottom left), 16 (top left, top right, bottom left, and bottom right), 18, 25 (top right), 28 (top left, top middle, top right, and bottom middle), 32, 36 (bottom left), 38, 39 (all), 41 (top and bottom left), 42 (bottom left and bottom right), 46 (right), 47 (top left and bottom), 53 (top), 55 (top left and right), 56 (bottom left), 60, 62 (bottom left), 66, 79 (top left), 82 (top middle), 87 (top left and right), 88 (top left and middle), 93 (top), 96 (top middle), 99 (top and bottom right), 101 (top right), 105 (top), 106, 112, 116 (bottom middle and right), 121 (top), 124, 127 (top), 132, 133 (top), 134, 135 (top right), 136 (top right and bottom left), 138, 139 (bottom right), 140, 141 (top left and right), 145 (bottom left and right), 147 (top), 148 (top left), 152, 156 (bottom right), 158, 159 (middle right and bottom), 160, 165 (top), 167 (bottom left)

Courtesy of Springtide Press Collection: pages ii, vi, 1, 7, 15 (top left), 21 (bottom), 22 (top left), 36 (top middle and bottom middle), 45 (bottom left), 46 (left), 62 (top middle), 67 (bottom left), 68 (bottom right), 76 (bottom middle), 88 (bottom left), 102 (bottom left), 108 (bottom left), 128 (top right and bottom right), 135 (top left), 142 (top right), 156 (top left, bottom left, and bottom middle), 167 (top right)

Courtesy of the Centers for Disease Control Public Health Image Library (PHIL): page 65 (bottom right)

Courtesy of the Emma Smith DeVoe Papers, Washington State Library. Photo by Chandler O'Leary: page 121 (bottom right)

Courtesy of the National Archives and Records Administration, Records of the US House of Representatives, Record Group 233, HR 55A-H28.3: page 165 (bottom left)

Courtesy of the National Archives and Records Administration: pages 33 (top left), 35 (top), 40, 113 (top), 125 (bottom), 127 (bottom right)

Courtesy of the National Digital Library of the US Fish and Wildlife Service: pages 65 (top), 67 (middle right), 68 (top right)

Courtesy of Wikimedia Commons: pages 22 (bottom middle), 33 (bottom right), 36 (bottom right), 45 (bottom right), 48 (top right), 52, 56 (top left and right), 80, 81 (bottom), 82 (top left), 85 (top), 88 (bottom right), 92, 93 (bottom right), 96 (top left and bottom middle), 105 (bottom), 107 (top), 108 (top middle, top left, and bottom right), 113 (bottom), 114 (all), 115 (all), 116 (top left), 119 (bottom), 128 (top middle and bottom middle), 136 (bottom right), 139 (top and bottom left), 146, 147 (bottom left), 148 (bottom middle and right), 153 (bottom left), 154, 155 (top), 159 (top), 161 (top and bottom left), 162 (top middle), 164, 167 (top left), 168 (top left, top middle, and bottom left)

Cover of the *Washington Women's Cook Book*, published by the Washington Equal Suffrage Association, 1909. Courtesy of the University of Washington Libraries, 20122341. Used with permission: page 118

Detail of photo of May Arkwright Hutton, c. 1906. Courtesy of the Northwest Museum of Arts & Culture, Eastern Washington State Historical Society. Used with permission: page 119 (top right)

Dutch embroidered matzoh cover, 1919. Courtesy of the United States Holocaust Memorial Museum, 2008.220.5: page 102 (top left)

Elizabeth Zimmermann photographed for *Knitting Without Tears*, 1971. Photo by Walter Sheffer. Courtesy of Meg Swansen, SchoolhousePress.com. Used with permission: page 84

"Endpaper Mitts" pattern by Eunny Jang. Photo and knitting by Chandler O'Leary: page 88 (top right)

EZ and Arnold Zimmermann. Photographer unknown. Courtesy of Meg Swansen, SchoolhousePress.com. Used with permission: page 85 (bottom right)

EZ describing her Sawtooth Border invention. Photo by Chris Swansen. Courtesy of Meg Swansen, SchoolhousePress.com. Used with permission: page 85 (bottom left)

Foss boathouse on the City Waterway, Tacoma, Washington, c. 1890. Courtesy of the Tacoma Public Library Northwest Room, 36417. Used with permission: page 45 (top)

Girl Up photo: girls in front of White House. Image courtesy of Girl Up, United Nations Foundation: page 20

"Grow Your Own, Can Your Own" US Office of War Information poster, 1943. Illustrated by Alfred Parker. Courtesy of the Northwestern University Library: page 35 (bottom left)

Illuminated *ketubah*, 1911. Courtesy of the Yale University Beinecke Rare Book & Manuscript Library, 2040851: page 102 (top middle)

Illuminated page from *Marvels of Things Created and Miraculous Aspects of Things Existing*, after original by al-Qazwīnī, Western India, 1537. Courtesy of the Islamic Medical Manuscripts at the National Library of Medicine: page 107 (bottom right)

Illustrated page of a child's diary written in a Swiss refugee camp, 1933 to 1944. Courtesy of the United States Holocaust Memorial Museum, 525.347. Used with permission: page 101 (bottom)

Illustrations by Chandler O'Leary: pages iii, 62 (bottom middle), 68 (top middle, bottom left, and bottom middle), 76 (top middle), 82 (bottom left and middle), 148 (bottom left), 162 (bottom left)

Imogen Cunningham, *Calla Lilly*, before 1929. ©2016 Imogen Cunningham Trust. Used with permission: page 73 (top)

Imogen Cunningham, *Frida Kahlo*, 1931. ©2016 Imogen Cunningham Trust. Used with permission: page 73 (bottom left)

Imogen Cunningham, *Self Portrait in Mirror, Hume*, 1934. ©2016 Imogen Cunningham Trust. Used with Permission: page 72

Kanji calligraphy by Hiroshi Oki: page 82 (bottom right)

*Monument to the Great Northern Migration*, by Alison Saar, 1996, Bronzeville, Chicago, Illinois. Photo by Carolyn Allen. Used with permission: page 27 (top right)

NASA Earth Observatory image of oil slick in the Gulf of Mexico, June 10, 2010. Created by Jesse Allen, using data provided courtesy of NASA/GSFC/METI/ERSDAC/JAROS, and US/Japan ASTER Science: page 67 (top)

National Women's Political Caucus pennant, autographed by Bella Azbug. From the private collection of Eli and Rochelle Gandour-Rood. Used with permission: page 5 (top)

Page from the diary of Rywka Lipszyc. Courtesy of the JFCS Holocaust Center at Jewish Family and Children's Services of San Francisco, the Peninsula, Marin and Sonoma Counties. Used with permission: pages 101 (top left) and 102 (bottom right)

Photo by Alexandra Alethea. Courtesy of Wikimedia Commons: page 48 (bottom middle)

Photo by Anderson Sady. Courtesy of Wikimedia Commons: page 22 (top right and bottom left).

Photo by Caitlin Harris. Courtesy of IPRC: page 94

Photo by Celtus. Courtesy of Wikimedia Commons: page 136 (top left)

Photo by Christopher J. Flynn. Courtesy of Wikimedia Commons: page 108 (top right)

Photo by Fanghong. Courtesy of Wikimedia Commons: page 156 (top middle)

Photo by Informationswiedergutmachung. Courtesy of Wikimedia Commons: page 100

Photo by Iramuthusamy. Courtesy of Wikimedia Commons: page 107 (bottom left)

Photo by Jane Carlin: page 181

Photo by John Cummings. Courtesy of Wikimedia Commons: page 93 (bottom left)

Photo by Kate Porter, Youth in Focus. Used with permission: page 74

Photo by Lionel Allorge. Courtesy of Wikimedia Commons: page 162 (top left)

Photo by Lubomir Čevela. Courtesy of Wikimedia Commons: page 76 (bottom left)

Photo by Marie-Lan Nguyen. Courtesy of Wikimedia Commons: page 148 (top middle)

Photo by Marsyas. Courtesy of Wikimedia Commons: page 145 (top)

Photo by Masur. Courtesy of Wikimedia Commons: page 147 (bottom right)

Photo by Michael O'Leary: page 171(bottom)

Photo by Miguel Hermoso Cuesta. Courtesy of Wikimedia Commons: page 144

Photo by Mirka Hokkanen: page 171 (top)

Photo by Rama. Courtesy of Wikimedia Commons: page 142 (top left)

Photo by Roger Russell. Used with permission: page 142 (bottom middle)

Photo by shakko. Courtesy of Wikimedia Commons: page 156 (top right)

Photo by Suzanne Moore: page 19 (top right)

Photo by Takkk. Courtesy of Wikimedia Commons: page 162 (bottom middle)

Photo by the Office of the Washington Secretary of State: page 120

Photo by Tony Webster. Courtesy of Wikimedia Commons: page 26

Photo by Triplebrook. Courtesy of Wikimedia Commons: page 25 (bottom)

Photo by Urban. Courtesy of Wikimedia Commons: page 36 (top left)

Photo of the Wall of Respect mural by William Walker, Chicago, Illinois (demolished 1971). Photo by Mark Rogovin. Courtesy of the University of Chicago Visual Resources Center and Mark Rogovin. Used with permission: page 27 (bottom)

Photos by Chandler O'Leary: pages 6, 7, 9, 16 (top middle), 22 (top middle), 28 (bottom right), 42 (top left, top middle, top right, and bottom middle), 48 (top middle, bottom left, and bottom right), 53 (bottom left), 62 (top left, top right, and bottom middle), 76 (top left, top right, and bottom right), 79 (top right), 81 (top left), 82 (top right), 87 (bottom), 88 (bottom middle), 95 (top left and right), 96 (top right), 108 (bottom middle), 116 (top middle), 122 (bottom middle and right), 168 (top right), 171 (bottom), 172, 173, 174

Photos by Jessica Spring: pages 48 (top left), 56 (bottom middle), 68 (top left), 102 (bottom middle), 116 (top right), 142 (bottom right), 148 (top right)

Photos by Shiori Oki. Used with permission: page 79 (bottom left and right)

Political illustration of Emma Goldman in the Anaconda Standard, September 22, 1901. Courtesy of Richard Gibson and the Butte (Montana) Archives: page 153 (top)

Posting signs to promote woman suffrage, Washington Equal Suffrage Association, Seattle, Washington, 1910. Photo by Asahel Curtis. Courtesy of the University of Washington Libraries, PH Coll 482. Used with permission: page 122 (top right)

Prints by Jessica Spring and Chandler O'Leary: pages viii, 21 (top left), 95 (bottom), 96 (bottom left), 121 (bottom left), 133 (bottom right), 159 (middle left)

Pulitzer Prize gold medal, designed by Daniel Chester French, 1917. Courtesy of the American Numismatic Society and Wikimedia Commons: page 161 (bottom right)

Rachel Carson at her microscope, c. 1962. Courtesy of the Yale University Beinecke Rare Book and Manuscript Library. Used with permission of the Rachel Carson Estate: page 64

Sarojini Naidu, c. 1940. Photographer unknown. Courtesy of the Museum of Art & Photography, India, PHY.03807. Used with permission: page 104

Sketchbook drawings by Chandler O'Leary: pages 21 (top right), 28 (bottom left), 73 (bottom right), 136 (top middle)

Star of David badge and Łódź Ghetto currency, 1939 to 1945. Courtesy of the United States Holocaust Memorial Museum, 2007.45.8; 2001.278.1; 1996.60.1: page 99 (bottom right)

Suffrage buttons, c. 1900 to 1910. From the Woman Suffrage Artifacts Collection at Kenneth Florey. Used with permission: page 41 (bottom right)

Supersisters Trading Card used with permission of Lois Rich and Barbara Egerman: page 125 (top left)

Texas Under Six Flags postcard, 1907. Courtesy of the University of Houston Library Historic Texas Postcards Collection: page 59 (top)

Thea Foss portrait. Courtesy of Foss Waterway Seaport. Used with permission: page 44

View from above the courtyard of al-Qarawiyyin Mosque, c. 1900. Image courtesy of Harvard University, Fine Arts Library, Special Collections: page 19 (bottom)

# About the Authors

❖ ❖ ❖

## CHANDLER O'LEARY

+ Born on October 30, 1981; spent her childhood moving around the United States
+ Spent a year in Italy studying art history and keeping sketchbooks
+ Received her BFA from the Rhode Island School of Design
+ Runs a small business called Anagram Press, specializing in illustration and lettering
+ Still keeps sketchbooks of her travels, and writes an illustrated travel blog called
  *Drawn the Road Again*

## JESSICA SPRING

+ Born on January 7, 1964, in Berkeley, California
+ Grew up in an extended family that included one dad, two moms, three sisters, and three
  grandmothers; now lives with her husband and son
+ Graduated with an English degree from Macalester College and an MFA at Columbia College
  Center for Book & Paper Arts
+ Teaches printing and book arts, with an emphasis on innovative techniques she calls
  "daredevil letterpress"
+ Designs, typesets, and prints artist books and broadsides at Springtide Press

The original Dead Feminists broadside series is a collaboration between Chandler O'Leary and Jessica Spring. The broadsides feature quotes by historical feminists, tied in with current political and social issues. Each limited-edition broadside was letterpress printed from hand-drawn lettering and illustrations. A portion of the proceeds of each piece was donated to a nonprofit cause that aligns with the issue highlighted by the artwork, in honor of the power of the press to change the world. Jessica and Chandler have released new broadsides on roughly a quarterly basis since the series began in 2008.

**DeadFeminists.com**

# About the Text

❖ ❖ ❖

The hand-lettered typography in both the broadsides and this book references the time and place in which each dead feminist lived and worked. Chandler found inspiration in a wide variety of sources, from Victorian circus posters to Mexican signage, from eighteenth-century colonial manuscripts to modern street graffiti, from Art Deco storefronts to sacred architecture. This book also highlights antique wood and metal type and image cuts at Springtide Press, as well as our own collections of unique ephemera.

The book was typeset in Adobe Garamond Pro, Futura, and Bodoni—digital versions of their historical metal counterparts.